THE TIMES WE LIVED IN

A trip through The Irish Times photographic archive

Arminta Wallace

IRISH TIMES BOOKS

Published by: The Irish Times Limited (Irish Times Books)
Design & Layout: Angelo McGrath

© The Irish Times Limited 2014

ISBN 978 0 9070 1140 8

There are no rules for good photographs;
there are only good photographs.
-Ansel Adams

The best-laid schemes o' Mice an' Men
Gang aft agley.
-Robert Burns

Introduction

When I was invited to start a weekly column in the Saturday magazine using photographs from The Irish Times archive, I had no idea what I was letting myself in for.

I got the picture, if you'll pardon the pun, pretty quickly. Imagine jumping into what you think is a swimming pool, only to find - oops! - it's actually a trampoline.

In the first month alone I found myself researching the Troubles, the Beef Tribunal and the Cold War. Bob Geldof and Lutrellstown Castle. Eamon de Valera and Garret FitzGerald and Mikhail Gorbachev.

Each week's article was to be just a couple of hundred words. I wanted them to be jewel-like miniatures. But behind those deceptively tiny finished articles lay a vast array of complex subject matter, about most of which I knew pitifully little - or less.

And that was just the words. The photographs were another universe again. It never occurred to me that there'd be a shortage of images - I've seen too many superb pictures in the pages of the paper, over the years, for that - but I swiftly realised that thanks to the march of newspaper and photographic technology, they're not always easy to get your hands on.

The word "archive" suggests something orderly, neat and predictable. But newspapers are notoriously unpredictable places. Negatives get misfiled, or go missing altogether. Prints get damaged. In the olden days, harassed sub-editors (myself included) thought nothing of taking a scissors to an image to make sure they got the exact crop they wanted. Thinking back on it, it raises the hairs on the back of my neck - but that's how it was.

These days the physical part of our photo archive is stored far from the newspaper's city-centre offices in an endless succession of dusty boxes, adding a further layer of intricacy and uncertainty.

Without the support and enthusiasm of Irene Stevenson, a trained librarian and archivist who can find her way around this arcane labyrinth with ease, I'd have bounced off The Times We Lived In trampoline after a couple of months, wiped my bloodied knees and limped away from the column as fast as I could go.

Instead, something surprising began to happen. Readers began to get in touch with comments, corrections and words of encouragement. Letters and emails arrived from Dingle and from Cambridge, from farmers and from academics, from lawyers and business people. The combination of text and image seemed to appeal to folks of all ages and backgrounds.

From an experimental seed, planted by the editor of The Irish Times magazine Orna Mulcahy and nurtured weekly by the magazine's production editor, Rachel Collins, and a lovely and observant team of features sub-editors, The Times We Lived In grew into a healthy plant.

The columns are still, in many ways, tales of the unexpected. From the outset we intended the images to be random - that is, not closely tied to current events or stories - all the better to surprise and delight readers as they arrive at the magazine's back page.

But we never set out to deliberately rescue the oldest pictures and give them new life in the newspaper's digital archive. That, literally, just happened. Wonderful pictures arrived out of the blue to surprise and delight us; and there are, we're quite sure, plenty more to come.

There's always a danger, publishing weekly columns all together in a book, that the text will be repetitive and tedious. In this case, we hope that the eloquence of the photographs will outweigh any inadequacy on the part of the words - and that readers will be tolerant of this writer's biases and weaknesses.

There are, by any scientific calculation, probably far too many pictures of children, musicians and the Zoo. Dublin streetscapes, particularly if they contain people, are another favourite. One of the latter, a view of Parnell Square, reminded me of the opening lines of a poem.

I invited readers to compose their own poem based on the image - and shouldn't have been surprised when a number of poems duly arrived by post and email.

Among them were a song-like "ode in light-hearted mode" from Joan Denihan from Castleknock, which included the lines:
Hostels aplenty for girls from the country
And dancing places to beat the band . . .
You could park your bike on the northern end
And hit the shops if you'd money to spend

From Prehen in Derry, Madeleine E M Coyle sent an atmospherically busy piece which began:
The days are never long enough,
So much to be done.
Maybe I could find the time
For an ice-cream at Forte's . . .

There isn't space here to thank all the people who have taken the trouble to write, but I would like to mention Ian Dickie from Belfast, who provided invaluable information about a photograph of a tow-horse on the Queen's Bridge; to Tim O'Neill and Alma Nowlan, who helped fill in the puzzle surrounding the names of a group of people on the steps of Marsh's Library in Dublin; to Monica Ward (nee Larkin) for sharing the background to a fantastic photograph of herself and her sisters; and, most recently, to Hugo Greene for telling the story of his mother Angela McCrea, who not only appeared in one of our best Zoo pictures but was also a published poet and winner of the Patrick Kavanagh award.

Details such as these, when we get hold of them, are added to the digital archive along with the images; a process of textual and contextual restoration for the photographs, in a way.

The last word, though, has to be for the Irish Times photographers whose dedication, expertise and humour combine to make these pictures so remarkable. I worked with many of them over the years, and can see their individual personalities reflected in their approach to shooting their subjects. Some, now retired, have been particularly supportive to the column - take a bow, Peter Thursfield and Jack McManus - but they are all, as indeed are our current crop of photographers and film-makers, outstanding professionals and extraordinary people.

The publication of this book celebrates three years of The Times We Lived In. We loved putting it together. We hope you enjoy it too.

Arminta Wallace

Thunder Road

Severe weather conditions may well be a regular feature of Irish life in a future dominated by climate change: but they've also been a feature of winters - and indeed summers - past. The photograph shows a woman in an optimistically sleeveless summer dress being helped by two CIE busmen, all of them up to their knees in water, on the Stillorgan Road. It's June 1963, and as the afternoon rush-hour reaches its peak, Dublin is hit by the mother of all thunderstorms. Or, as the front-page story for Wednesday, June 12th puts it, "In the wake of the most damaging thunderstorms to have hit Dublin in years, floodwaters raged through the city suburbs last night, causing untold damage to property and threatening life in a residential area from Merrion gates to Stillorgan." During the height of the storm, a young man from Fairview, Kevin Baker, was thrown high into the air on Pearse Street as a blast of lightning hit the footpath where he walked. He was treated for burns and shock in St Patrick Dun's hospital. In Kilmacud, a doctor was watching the floods from the apparent safety of his own home "when the swirling waters smashed down three neighbouring walls and swept five feet high, like a tidal wave, into his house". People were marooned in houses containing up to four feet of water; many more were stuck for hours in massive traffic-jams. "Motorists," the story explains, "had a nightmare time. The waters deepened without seeming to do so, and many drivers who thought it safe to take a chance regretted the impulse later." It wasn't all bad, mind you, if the smiles of the three people in the photograph are anything to go by. Still. Irish summers, eh? Makes the winter we've been having look like child's play. So far . . . **Published 07/01/2012**

Published June 12th, 1963
Photograph by Jimmy McCormack

Satire with bite

Ah, the glory days of political satire. With Meryl Streep's pallid version of the Iron Lady currently gracing our cinema screens, it's salutary to remind ourselves that once upon a time, popular commentary came in more spiky varieties. And few were spikier than Terence Alan Milligan, aka "Spike"; poet, jazz musician, writer, humanitarian and comedian, who was bipolar before anybody had ever heard of the disorder, and who decided in the middle of the 1960s that he was Irish. This, despite a classic colonial childhood in India, a spell of Royal Artillery service that saw him wounded during the second World War, and a healthy if often controversial career on British television. Having availed of an Irish passport and with strong Irish family connections, he visited Ireland often. In the autumn of 1982, his Dublin show *Spike Milligan and Friends* was a sellout. He is pictured with one of the "friends": sadly, the caption doesn't record the accompanying dialogue, but it's a safe bet that it isn't complimentary, politically correct or - heaven forbid - pallid. The clues are in the expression on the Thatcher puppet's face and the delightfully dishevelled head of her supposedly ancient "admirer". A year earlier, Milligan had been castigated for his characterisation of Thatcher - in a play called *The Bedsittingroom* - as a deceased parrot. For all of these reasons, or perhaps just for lack of space, the photograph wasn't published at the time. We think it's high time to bring it out now. After Milligan died in 2002, a psychologist by the name of Richard Wiseman (don't you just love it?) conducted a poll of 100,000 people to establish the funniest gag ever written. Milligan came out on top with a typically black gem from a 1950s *Goon Show* sketch based on two hunters in the woods, an emergency service operator, and a gunshot. Too lengthy to repeat here, but you'll find it online if you need it. Genius. It never goes out of fashion. **Published 07/01/2012**

Published September 20th, 1982
Photograph by Eddie Kelly

Richard Nixon's Visit

When Richard Nixon visited Ireland in October 1970, it's a safe bet that his aim was to make a name for himself as an international statesman and diplomat. Thing weren't going well for the US on the world stage; the war in Vietnam was dragging on; ongoing peace talks in Paris had long since run out of steam. Surely a jaunt to his Irish roots, near Timahoe in Co Kildare, would result in cheering peasantry and smiling faces? After all, it had worked well for John F Kennedy just seven years earlier: and the Irish always put on a good show for visiting dignitaries. As our photograph of the Nixon cavalcade shows, there were people in Ireland who were happy to shake the US president's hand. The gesture of the garda in the car nearest the photographer, however, could be interpreted as saying a lot about the wider verdict on the visit. The visit was opposed not just by those who disagreed with the war in Vietnam, but by all kinds of groups, from the Irish Third World Group to the Irish Campaign for Greek Democracy, which deplored the visit "in the light of the resumption of US arms shipments to the Greek military junta". And despite the folksy welcome speech from then taoiseach Jack Lynch, it was clear to most commentators that it was US money for capital development projects that Ireland really wanted to attract. The front-page story in this newspaper on the day Nixon arrived in Ireland spoke of rising unemployment due to a drop in emigration and fewer jobs in the farming sector. Two years later, there would be more smiling and waving as Nixon made his historic visit to China. But history had a trick up its sleeve; 1972 was also the year of the Watergate scandal, and by the summer of 1974 the man known to posterity as Tricky Dicky would be forced into an ignominious resignation. So that garda, whoever he was, was spot on with his apparent thumb's down. **Published - 21/01/2012**

Published: October 5th 1970
Photograph by Jimmy McCormack

581-800

GARDA

Still waters run deep

They were easily the world's most glamorous couple. And in this picture - taken at Dublin airport as they wait to board a flight to Munich - star quality oozes from every pore: he in threads so immaculate you can see, well, every thread; she swathed in fur, her hair piled, diva-style, on top of her head. But the image has a sombre, almost haunted quality - with good reason, as we shall see. What were Richard Burton and Elizabeth Taylor doing in Ireland in the first place? It was hardly mid-1960s Hollywood A-list territory. But Burton was starring in the film *The Spy Who Came In From The Cold*. This chilliest of Cold War thrillers is set in Berlin - but the film-makers decided that our very own Smithfield Market was a dead ringer for the area around Checkpoint Charlie. A generous helping of snow, and uniformly leaden Irish skies during the course of the shoot, helped the buttoned-up atmosphere along nicely. Claire Bloom was Burton's leading lady on this occasion. Nevertheless the entire Burton-Taylor entourage moved into The Gresham on O'Connell Street for 10 weeks, taking over a whole floor of the hotel with their four children, a nanny, a maid and a pet bush-baby - which regularly caused minor mayhem by knocking over vases and lamps, climbing up the curtains and hiding in the pipes of the bathroom ceiling. Such was daily life in celebrity-land. Real life, however, was hardly kind to the world's most famous movie star and the world's leading classical actor during their stay in Ireland. Just before they arrived, the 17-year-old son of Taylor's French chauffeur, Gaston Sanz, was shot dead in a fairground in Paris; and Sanz was embroiled in tragedy once again when, on March 3rd, he was at the wheel of Taylor's Rolls-Royce when it struck and killed a pedestrian, Alice Brian, on the Stillorgan dual carriageway. Small wonder that, in the photograph, Burton looks tentative to the point of apologetic while Taylor - the famous eyes enormous under elaborately coiffed brows - is sipping a sober glass of water. Champagne time, it wasn't. They returned to Dublin to give evidence at the inquest. But until her death last March at the age of 79, Taylor never visited Ireland again. **Published - 28/01/2012**

Published: April 5th, 1965
Photograph by Jimmy McCormack

Moore Street

It has been a favourite with Dublin shoppers for more years than even "auld Mr Brennan" would care to remember. Moore Street takes its name from Henry Moore, the earl of Drogheda, who was from a 16th-century planter family which owned the land around St Mary's Abbey, off what is now Capel Street. Once upon a time this part of the city was alive with street markets: the Rotunda Market, Taaffe's Market, the Norfolk Market and Anglesea Market, which sold second-hand clothes, shoes and furniture. But in 1972 these were all removed, and the Ilac Centre was built in their place. The stalls along Moore Street have traditionally been manned - if that's the right word - by feisty Dublin women who stand for no nonsense from passersby but are always ready to do a deal for their regular customers. Nowadays, of course, the voices are as likely to be from Africa as from Dublin; as is much of the edible produce. Our photograph, which dates from 1955, shows Miss Vera Colgan and Mrs Mary Colgan at their well-stocked fruit and vegetable stall. The photographer's name is not recorded, nor is the reason for the shot. It seems not to have been published, perhaps because it shows what was, at the time, an unremarkable city scene. But Moore Street did hit the headlines that year. On Saturday July 23rd, 1955, *The Irish Times* carried a front-page report to the effect that a 16-year-old boy called John Barrett had found a highly unfamiliar black and white striped insect on one of the street's stalls. He wasn't sure whether it had come from a case of Spanish greengages or a crate of onions, also from Spain - but he was pretty sure it wasn't kosher. Inspectors from the Department of Agriculture duly confirmed that the insect was the dreaded Colorado beetle, a virulent predator of potato crops that is still a quarantined pest in the EU. The dreaded development bug has proved more difficult to control. Number 16 Moore Street, the house where leaders of the 1916 Rising met after fleeing the GPO, has been designated a national monument along with the houses on either side. The Save Moore Street group wants the area restored and preserved, but planning permission has already been given for another massive shopping centre which would obliterate many of the laneways that surround the historic terrace. Wouldn't you love to know what the Colgan ladies would have had to say on the matter? **Published - 04/02/2012**

Published: 1955

Taking the (Sir) Michael

Our photographer David Sleator snapped these two Michaels - no, wait, not just two Michaels but two Sir Michaels, better known as Michael Caine and Michael Gambon - at a press conference held at The Four Seasons Hotel in Dublin in May 2003. The occasion was the morning after the premiere of the film *The Actors*, in which Caine and Dylan Moran play two not-so-eminent actors who plan to con a retired gangster out of half a million; the film also stars Gambon as an individual who goes by the name of, um, Barreller. If this photograph is anything to go by, the two Sir Michaels got on like the proverbial house on fire; though why they have matching poses of hands clasped on their knees is anyone's guess. Perhaps it's a sub-conscious reference to the fact that Caine's role in the movie required him to get into drag - at which point it was, apparently, discovered that he has absolutely fabulous legs. Not many people knew that at the time: certainly not the film's director, Conor McPherson, who had planned to use a female stunt double for the drag scenes. Caine's 70-year-old legs turned out to be so attractive, the director declared, that the double wasn't needed after all. At this point, we might all be forgiven for wondering whether some serious (Sir) Michael isn't being taken at this press conference. Caine's laughter, however, is surely genuine. And if this image did make you smile - even a little - you could do worse than to get yourself along to Stargazing in Dublin, a photographic exhibition running on the top floor at the Stephen's Green Shopping Centre in Dublin as part of the Jameson Dublin International Film Festival. Assembled from a wide range of sources including RTÉ, freelance agency archives and *The Irish Times*, the exhibition features 100 photographs taken over a 60-year period and celebrates "the moments when a little bit of Hollywood stardust was sprinkled over the capital". Among the celebrities captured during visits to Dublin are Mia Farrow, Britt Ekland, Paul Newman, Walt Disney and, of course, the two Sir Michaels.
Published 11/02/2012

Published May 8th, 2003
Photograph by David Sleator

11

Post Office Girls

Ah, the uniforms of yesteryear. Just 12 months ago, there was great rejoicing in the land as An Post staff members took delivery of their new urban-chic outfits. Now a familiar presence on the country's highways and byways, the studiously unstructured beanies and baseball caps, shorts and gilets have been declared to be more practical and hard-wearing than the uniforms they replaced - not to mention better supplied with pockets in which to carry the mobile phones, keys and "postbox scanning equipment" without which no self-respecting 21st-century postman or woman could effectively operate. Our photo, however, reveals that in the spring of 1987, a previous generation of postal workers was also stepping into the future in distinctly sprightly fashion, showing off its cutting-edge costume with obvious delight. And why not? The 1987 An Post uniform was designed by Paul Costelloe, who went on to design landmark work-gear for - among others - British Airways, Sainsbury's supermarkets and Formula One team The Orange Arrows. It was, at the time, greeted as a huge improvement on the highly masculine pullovers and old-style trousers that had preceded it - though, looking back, the peaked caps, striped ties and tailored lines are almost quaintly natty and retain a distinctly military feel. It's surely no accident that the photograph features four particularly smart-looking female postal operatives. Perhaps An Post was emphasising Costelloe's female-friendly silhouette in order to attract more women into the job. Two decades on, however, postwomen are still sufficiently unusual in certain parts of Ireland for the *Mayo News* to feature the county's first of the species, Cathy Scanlon, on its front page in September 2011. We don't have names for the four postwomen in our photo. Respect, though. Never mind the marauding dogs, intransigent letterboxes and incorrect addresses which can make the most determined postman or woman weep: it can't have been easy for them to carry out that cheesy pose - part hokey-cokey, part step-it-out-Mary, part eerie *Riverdance* preview - and still keep smiling. **Published - 21/01/2012**

Published: March 24th, 1987
Photograph by Paddy Whelan

Jail birds

The sign, you might think, says it all. The Swinging Sixties are nearly over, yet Irish women are still wearing placards on their backs to the effect that they know their place in the pecking order - and it isn't at the top. But take a closer look. The woman on the extreme right has the confidence of an aristocrat at a garden party, complete with hat, handbag and leather gloves. The woman wearing the sign, meanwhile, is straight out of a 1960s fashion shoot: her check immaculate, her waist nipped, her heels impressively high for a woman on a National Farmers' Association protest march. These are top-notch ladies. No wonder the newspaper sellers are gawking. The main report explains that 2,000 women turned up in Merrion Square to protest at the incarceration of more than 40 farmers in Portlaoise and Limerick jails "for refusing to pay fines and sign bonds arising out of an NFA road blockade". They have come specifically to plead with the taoiseach, Jack Lynch, to release their husbands and sons; but also to register a more general protest at "the sad state" of provincial Ireland. Alongside that suitably sober account is a colour story by Mary Maher - one of the leading feminist voices in Ireland at the time - which captures the mercurial mood of the day. Maher describes how, detained by a line of gardaí determined to keep them away from the Dáil, the women vented their frustration on a pale green Ford Consul, which had innocently driven into the midst of the fray. A "stout grey-haired woman" sat on the car's bonnet, to the delight of the protesters, who called out, "Good woman, Mrs Baxter!" and explained that two members of the Baxter family were in jail. The driver of the car was not amused. She drove off in tears, Maher concludes, "her car now plastered with NFA stickers. The child in the back seat continued to sleep through it all." The protesting women eventually got to meet the taoiseach. But although three of the men were released on the following day, the rest of the farmers spent five weeks in jail. They were finally freed on June 12th.
Published 25/02/2012

Published June 2nd, 1967
Photograph by Gordon Standing

Write and left

It was a joyous day: the wedding, at Kildare Street registry office in Dublin, of the writer Christy Brown. "The groom," reads the caption, "who overcame severe physical handicap by learning to write and paint with his left foot, signed the register in the same manner." The 40-year-old Brown, author of *My Left Foot* and *Down All the Days* was a celebrity. Crowds of well-wishers and friends greeted his arrival at the registry office with his 27-year-old bride, Mary Carr; among the guests at the wedding reception were the film producer Kevin McClory; actors Richard Harris, Niall Toibin and Anna Manahan, and Charles Haughey, TD. The caption concludes with the information that "the honeymoon will be spent at a villa in the Bahamas loaned by Mr McClory, and the couple will live in the groom's recently-built house in Rathcoole, Co Dublin". Nowadays most people know Christy Brown through the 1989 film of *My Left Foot* which stars Daniel Day-Lewis. It portrays Brown's early life as the 10th of 22 children born to a Dublin bricklayer, and his struggle to express himself as a poet, novelist and painter despite severe physical disability due to cerebral palsy. The film ends with Brown sharing a bottle of champagne with his nurse, Mary Carr - and a final caption tells the audience that they married in 1972, leaving the viewer with a distinct impression of "happy ever after". Real life was, as ever, to prove somewhat more complex. An authorised biography published in 2007 claimed that the marriage alienated Brown from his family and that Carr, who was an alcoholic, neglected the writer during their nine years of married life. "I felt sad when I found these things out, because he was a genius," the book's author, Georgina Hambleton, said. "He is comparable to Patrick Kavanagh and Brendan Behan and if he had been in a positive relationship with someone who fostered that intellect, he would have produced even better books." Christy Brown died in 1981, and Mary Carr in 2006. **Published - 03/03/2012**

Published: October 6th, 1972
Photograph by Pat Langan

18

Infection control

It has a wonderfully sinister feel, this photograph. So uncompromising is the uniformed official's expression that he might be ushering people across the river to Hades instead of up a ramp into Dublin airport. The machine at his feet has a strange, sci-fi look. And the group of travellers with their backs to the camera are hunched and wary as they head off into a swirl of mist which wouldn't be out of place in a Sherlock Holmes movie. Talk about capturing the zeitgeist. Gordon Standing's page-one shot conveys with terrific immediacy the prevailing mood in the winter of 1967. A major outbreak of foot-and-mouth disease had been under way in the UK for more than a month. The number of infected animals was mounting - more than 100,000 cattle and 40,000 sheep - and the Minister for Agriculture Neil Blaney decided it was time to impose some serious restrictions. Everyone entering Ireland from the UK was to be disinfected - hence the clouds of spray at Dublin airport - and air and shipping services announced that there would be no extra services for Christmas, presumably to dissuade people from travelling. All fairs were banned, and no one from the UK was allowed to visit Irish marts, co-ops, meat factories or creameries on pain of a fine or even a six-month prison sentence. The GAA cancelled all fixtures for the first weekend in December, and international sporting events were also affected. "If we don't get co-operation from the public or if the disease comes close to us, so that it appears that we cannot avoid getting it, then we will actively consider the closing of our ports," was the minister's grim pronouncement. No wonder the people in the photo seem so - pardon the pun - cowed. Maybe they're just cold. Or keeping their heads down to avoid getting a gob-ful of disinfectant. With hindsight, though, it's impossible to see this picture without thinking of the hellish images of 2001, when - following our most recent outbreak of the disease - some seven million sheep and cattle were slaughtered in the UK, and their carcasses burned on giant bonfires. Foot and mouth, sadly, appears to be one of our culture's most reliable sources of nightmarish iconography. **Published -17/03/2012**

Published November 30th, 1967
Photograph by Gordon Standing

Amazing Grace

Okay, it's great living in a republic and everything. But sometimes, don't you wish we had a couple of those oh-so-posey formal/royal portraits stashed away in our civic cupboard? Turns out we do. If there was such a thing as Irish royalty, it would surely have to include Dev and Grace Kelly - and here's the photographic proof. The first official State visit by royalty to Ireland since the days of Edward VIII nearly got rained off in June 1961 when the plane carrying Prince Rainier and Princess Grace of Monaco was delayed by low cloud and drizzle. The remainder of the visit, however, was a glittering success. Not too surprising, perhaps, considering the princess's pedigree; a Lovely Girl of Irish descent, from an observant Catholic family, who - having made it big in such Hollywood movies as *High Noon*, *Rear Window* and *Dial M for Murder* - proceeded to make off into the sunset with one of Europe's richest men. In fairness to their Serene Highnesses, they appeared to be game for pretty much anything on their Irish visit: the opening concert of the Dublin International Festival of Music and the Arts at Croke Park, a Red Cross Party at the Zoo. The biggest gig, though, was an evening event at Áras an Uachtaráin. Our front-page picture shows the President and Sinéad Bean De Valera with the prince and princess as they prepared to get stuck into the serious business of exchanging orders and medals and such-like. All are in full stiff-upper-lip mode, but Princess Grace steals the show. Her dress apparently artless, her posture pitch-perfect, she brings a touch of vividness to what must have been a pretty starchy diplomatic function. Sadly, we have no further details of that beautiful ballgown. By contrast, this paper's coverage of the Croke Park concert tells us that the movie-star-turned-princess arrived at the Hogan Stand wearing a theatre coat of bright violet wool, and that shortly after she took her seat she wrapped a scarf of "pale tulip-leaf green" loosely around her face. Predictably, this fine gossamer garment wasn't sufficient to keep the Irish evening breezes at bay - so the ever-practical Grace produced a grey mink stole and wrapped up, movie-star style. It was a touch of class which must, for a few magical seconds, have made of Croke Park the perfect setting for a presence more regal, in truth, than royal. **Published - 24/03/2012**

Published: June 12th, 1961

Peace on track

You'd never guess, from the exuberant expressions and obvious delight of this happy band of people, that they were working to promote cross-Border co-operation. You'd think they were just having a party. But then, there always was something of a party atmosphere around the Peace Train project. Which is not to say that it didn't have an entirely serious purpose. When the first peace trains ran on the weekend of October 28th, 1989, IRA bomb alerts had closed the railway line between Belfast and Dublin for 50 days in the previous five months, causing a major disruption to passenger and freight traffic. It also caused a major pain in the ass for anyone who had reason to travel between the two cities. The journey almost always - at some point - involved the tedious business of getting off the (warm) train and on to a (cold) waiting bus. Among those thus discombobulated on a regular basis was the writer and *Irish Times* columnist Sam McAughtry, who became the chairman of the Northern Peace Train committee; his Southern counterpart was the historian John de Courcy Ireland. There was to be no mercy even for the peace train's maiden voyage, which was disrupted when a telephoned bomb alert closed the line from Newry to Dundalk overnight. Undeterred, many of the passengers spent the night on board at Portadown station. Happily, the call proved to be a hoax. Our photo shows a scene from the fourth Peace Train event in 1992, when 1,000 people travelled on a shopping trip designed as a gesture of support for the people of Belfast. The merry travellers in the picture are members of a peace group from Portrane, Co Dublin. The return fare was a symbolic £1, and some Belfast shops did one-to-one exchange on the punt for the day. Taking a wild guess, the smiles and gestures of triumph have nothing to do with this temporary fiscal policy. The obviously genuine jubilation of these purveyors of peace is all the more moving in the context of the recent po-faced pontification about whether it is, after all, quite proper to go shopping on the "wrong" side of the Border any more.
Published -31/03/2012

Published March 2nd, 1992
Photograph by Paddy Whelan

Heroes and heroin

'DRUG PUSHERS are MURDERERS," reads the placard - a grim message which appears to be totally at odds with the beatific smile of the child who is carrying it. But for the people involved in the protest march - which took place on the Leap Year day of February 29th, 1984 - that, pretty much, is the whole story right there. It was the residents of St Teresa's Gardens who, frustrated by the open and constant sale of drugs in their area, began Dublin's anti-drugs movement in the early 1980s. Pushers Out protests quickly spread across the city to Ballymun, Finglas, Ballyfermot, Tallaght, Coolock, Cabra, Crumlin and Clondalkin. The campaign has subsequently been described - in a 2005 memoir by the activist Andre Lyder - as "one of the most significant social movements to emerge from Dublin's working-class communities during the 1980s and 1990s". At the time, however, there was a lot of grumbling, not to say hostility, from officialdom - and from certain sections of the media, which caricatured the movement as a front for republican paramilitarism, vigilantism and political ambition. The peaceful demonstration shown in this photograph, however, was described in an editorial in this newspaper as "one of the most persuasive seen for a long time". More than 1,000 people took part, a significant proportion of whom - the editorial continues - "were women pushing prams, with other children of walking age trudging along. "There was even a family dog, tied by a leash to one pram." If the protestors' demeanour was eloquent, even more so was the letter they delivered to the then taoiseach, Dr Garrett FitzGerald, and the minister for health, Michael Noonan. "We are not vigilantes," it began. "We are concerned parents; we are young people against drugs; we are determined old people; we are innocent." They certainly look like all of those things. Good humour radiates not just from the little girl with the placard but the woman wearing glasses to her right, and the woman with the big collar and even bigger 1980s perm walking behind. Buggies and prams add to the air of genial chaos. All that's missing from the image is that protesting dog. **Published - 07/04/2012**

Published: March 1st, 1984
Photograph by Kevin McMahon

25

Back to the future

'One man and his screen went to mow a meadow . . ." In the spring of 1999, the approaching millennium had us all recklessly predicting what the brave new post-2000 world might have in store. Were we worried about what was coming down the line? Yes, we were. Were we right? Well, not entirely. The strange, quixotic mood of the time is encapsulated in this shot of the erstwhile Carlow County Secretary of the Irish Farmers' Association, Aidan Byrne, hard at work on his computer. In the middle of a field. It's an image that could have come right out of the madder regions of *Monty Python's Flying Circus*. Remember the naked organist who used to pop up every so often, so to speak, in bizarre locations? Happily Mr Byrne remains fully - even sensibly - clothed as photographer Pat Langan captures him on his home turf of Clonegal against the backdrop of the softly rolling Blackstairs Mountains. The article, entitled "Farmer finds harvest on the internet" focuses on two farmers who have abandoned careers on the land. One is Paddy Berridge, who has recently founded Carrigbyrne Farmhouse Cheeses. The other is Mr Byrne - who explains that, though he studied agriculture to the highest levels and acquired a diploma in farm management as well as completing a six-month stint on a scholarship in New Zealand, he can't make enough money on his 35-acre farm to support his wife and two children. He has, therefore, turned to electronic publishing with his company Internet Publishing Services, creating and designing websites and . . . well, that sort of thing. To the rest of us, for whom - in 1999 - the internet was still a pretty obscure entity, he might as well have been stepping off the edge of the known world. From the vantage point of now, on the other hand, his computer has the look of a digital dinosaur. As it turned out, there were some spectacularly successful years to come for people in the IT business. As for the cheesemakers of Ireland they, too, were fruitful and multiplied. Is there a moral in the story? Maybe it's just that wise old line, "And now for something completely different . . ."
Published -14/04/2012

Published February 24th 1999
Photograph by Pat Langan

Euro visions

And we think Jedward's hairdos are scary? They're mild, frankly, compared to Michelle Rocca's curly-wurly perm and Pat Kenny's quiff - multiplied and magnified in our photo to nightmarishly outsized dimensions on the electronic wall behind their woolly heads. In April 1988, Johnny Logan having conquered Belgium the previous year with *Hold Me Now*, RTÉ was gearing up to host the Eurovision for the second time in a decade. Not only that, but we Irish had decided that the contest was quaint and outdated. Video producer Declan Downey was brought in to revamp the show for a younger generation, and the RDS stage was duly dominated by the Philips Vidiwall; "a revolutionary, high-tech set that looks", an *Irish Times* report noted, "like Steven Spielberg's soundstage for *Close Encounters of the Third Kind*". Well, quite. There was far more excitement over the Vidiwall than there was over our 1988 Eurovision entry, Jump the Gun's piano ballad *Take Him Home*. There was, naturally, a bit of mild hoo-ha about the cost of it all - though the show's executive director, Liam Miller, stoutly maintained that RTÉ had spent as much on the Eurovision as it would on "one hour of high-quality drama or several years of *Dempsey's Den*". Just in case you're wondering whether the station had decided to save money by disguising Rocca and Kenny as ordinary, everyday 1980s commuters, fear not. Our photo was taken at a rehearsal. On the night, Pat was dolled-up like a waiter at a Michelin-starred restaurant, complete with silver bow-tie. Michelle, meanwhile - as befitted the futuristic theme for the night that was in it - was dressed as a character from *Star Wars*, her perm sprayed solidly into a fetching Tellytubbies-style aerial thingummibob. In the end, it all went went swimmingly. Jump the Gun achieved a respectable eighth place and it was left to Austria to snag the traditional "nul points". The half-time entertainment was a snazzy new video from a young Irish band by the name of Hothouse Flowers. The winner? Switzerland's Celine Dion, with the ruthlessly upbeat *Ne Partez Pas Sans Moi* and a curly-wurly perm of her own. Oh, those Eurovisions of the past. Jedward are just regular dudes by comparison. **Published -21/04/2012**

Published: April 26th, 1988
Photograph by Matt Kavanagh

Party lines

There's something about the expression "garden party" which sets some people's teeth on edge - while others reach unhesitatingly for their parasols and straw boaters.

This study of the 1992 garden party at Trinity College, Dublin has something of the same divided loyalties. The pair on the left of the picture are wearing rebellious Gothic black. The man gazes lugubriously at the camera; his companion's head is turned defiantly away. On the right, by contrast, two women in white glow in the summer sunshine like a couple of lilies, all smiles and frills, gloves and heels. If you're still not sure which side of the garden-party debate you're on - a tooth-grinder? a straw boater? - have a quick read of these opening sentences from Katherine Mansfield's short story *The Garden Party*. "They could not have had a more perfect day for a garden-party if they had ordered it. Windless, warm, the sky without a cloud. The gardener had been up since dawn, mowing the lawns and sweeping them, until the grass and the dark flat rosettes where the daisy plants had been seemed to shine. As for the roses . . . Hundreds, yes, literally hundreds, had come out in a single night; the green bushes bowed down as though they had been visited by archangels. . ." Teeth on edge yet? You should read the whole story. It's not all champagne and cucumber sandwiches. There's quite a sting in the tale; not unlike the one administered by Peter Thursfield in his gently subversive image. As for the people who can be seen milling around in the background of the picture, well, they look a lot more like the rest of us: neither black nor white, just shades of garden-variety grey. But hey. Back here in the spring of good old 2012, summer is on the way. So even if you haven't had your invite to the garden party at Trinners this year; or Buck House; or the Sarkozy bash at the Palais de l'Elysée on Bastille Day, you can still look forward to sitting outdoors, of a long and balmy evening, with a glass of wine and a bag of crisps. Garden parties don't have to be what they used to be. **Published -28/04/2012**

Published February 24th 1999
Photograph by Peter Thursfield

31

Let's dance

'It's holiday (Camp) Dance Time!" croons the headline on the entertainment page of the Time Pictorial magazine. It's June 1954. The summer dance season is on the horizon. Eager young Dubliners are polishing up their winkle-pickers. Over the coming months, many will flock to band venues by the seaside - the Red Island camp in Skerries, in north Dublin, and Bray's Bar-B ballroom just over the border in Co Wicklow. At Red Island a bandleader by the name of Jack Ruane is challenging the popularity of Tin Pan Alley with his arrangements of Danny Boy and Cottage by the Lee. There's a buzz in Bray, too: a new singer has joined the Johnnie Butler Band. Our photo shows Pat Montana being introduced to the orchestra's drummer, Johnnie Butler Junior, by the bandleader, old JB himself. X Factor, nothing. The Bar-B represents Pat Montana's shot at the big-time; he has just quit his job as a call-boy at the Theatre Royal to try and make it as a singer. He looks awkward in his spanking new outfit, half lonesome cowboy, half overgrown boy scout. He also looks incredibly baby-faced - as, indeed, does the 18-year-old drummer. Between them they hold the orchestra's future in their hands. If you're going to keep discerning dancers on the floor, your drummer and your singer need to be first-rate - especially now, when musical change is in the air. Is there an anxious edge to the smile of proud dad Johnnie Butler Senior? Just below our photo, the column *Dancing Times* - by the tireless Dancalot - notes that "the really beautiful colour changing in the lighting system on the Crystal bandstand" has created "a really romantic atmosphere for dancing at the South Anne Street rendezvous". In his Clark Gable moustache and dark suit, Butler senior already looks old-fashioned compared to the shining young faces on either side of him. By the summer of 1954, the song which will change the face of popular music forever is already in the can; by the summer of 1955, Bill Haley and the Comets will be all the rage, their recording of *Rock Around The Clock* nudging the Glenn Miller big band from the top of the dance charts. But not in the Bar-B. Not yet.
Published -05/05/2012

Published June 19th, 1954
Photograph by Dermot Barry

Girl power

Celebrities under the hammer? Nowadays the phrase has a relentlessly red-top ring, but on this photographic occasion it was not only good-humoured, but in a good cause as well. At a charity auction in aid of Rehab at the Shelbourne Hotel in Dublin, a selection of glitterati of the day were offered for sale - including the three women featured in our photograph. On the left, the young Biddy White-Lennon would already have been familiar to Irish telly-watchers for her role as Maggie in *The Riordans*. In pole position in the centre of the picture is the rally driver Rosemary Smith, sporting a short-sleeved fun fur worn over - and watch out for this look to be revived any day now, folks - a long-sleeved shirt. And look at those earrings: she wasn't wearing those while whizzing around the racetrack at Monte Carlo. On the right is the Texaco sports star of the year for 1973, Mary Tracey, who was to hold the Irish records for the 800 metres, 1,500 metres and 3,000 metres until 1976 - and who did it all, this photo suggests, while in possession of the best-behaved wavy haircut this side of Kevin Keegan. It's a standard social column sort of image. But whether the photographer was aware of it or not (probably not) he was snapping three women who were highly visible and influential in Ireland in the 1970s. All three made for pretty impressive role models for a generation of Irish women, making a go of it in high-profile areas which had traditionally been dominated by men. Smith, in particular, carved her name with pride in a sport which - even now - regards women as decorative appendages rather than plausible participants. Tracey was one of the first batch of celebrity female athletes, a species which, as the current batch of Olympic hopefuls demonstrates, is up and running. But it's White-Lennon who takes the gold medal. She may look distinctly ill at ease in the the photo, but in the quarter-century since The Riordans was axed, she has confidently reinvented herself as a chef, food expert and author of a plethora of bestselling cookbooks. Recipe for success? You'd better believe it. **Published -12/05/2012**

Published May 8th, 1973
Photograph by Paddy Whelan

35

Final dispensation

It was a pearl among pharmacies. It had been on the go since 1897. But in the summer of 1975, JJ Graham's on Westmoreland Street closed its doors for the last time. "And now even Graham's is gone," reads the somewhat exasperated headline on an elegiac story by Elgy Gillespie. Gillespie writes that the first sale in the pharmacy's prescription book was for a pomade for a client on Fitzwilliam Square, cost one shilling (which is akin to Crème de la Mer skin-care prices nowadays). Almond hand cream was made out of whole unpeeled almonds. Graham's also made its own toothpaste - from soap powder, camphor and precipitated chalk - while its famously foul-tasting hangover cure is revealed as "a compound of bromivalarium and Alka Seltzer". The photo shows the pharmacy's dispensing staff in its final days of operation. Standing behind the counter are JJ Connaughton and Edward Ryan; in the front row, from left to right, are EM Flynn, the owner JJ Walsh, Anne Kehoe and Elizabeth Egan. They smile obligingly for the photographer, though JJ Walsh, in particular, has a slightly distracted air; hardly surprising, as the building had been owned by two generations of Walsh's before himself. Edward Ryan had worked in the shop for 41 years. Arriving there at the age of 18 as an apprentice, he was excused the usual £50 training fee because he had already served one year in his father's country chemist shop. He must surely have been impressed by the art nouveau interior of his new workplace, with its mahogany shelving and elaborate upper tier, all gilt, curlicues, cockle-shells and Corinthian pillars. In her article Gillespie mourns the loss of the "long drawers for quills, and the long shelves of belljars . . . Oh, those bottles, those endless rows inscribed from LIG: ARS all the way to PHD IODI - where will they go now?" she asks. Not into the glossy new EBS building which replaced the pharmacy, that's for sure. The EBS, of course, has now moved out. Such is the prescription for life in a city centre. **Published -26/05/2012**

Published: June 10th, 1975
Photograph by Tommy Collins

Beardy twins

Regardless of how Robbie Keane's hamstring holds up or whether Mesut Ozil turns out to be the new Zinedine Zidane, the best thing about the Euro 2012 tournament - bar none - is the prospect of having the Après Match TV sketch show back in footballing action. They've scored so many memorable goals over the years. Remember the time they did the entire commentary on the play-off match between "the Turkans and the South Koreans"? One of their most cherished series of sketches, though, has to be "The Three Joe Duffys", in which a trio of beardy, bespectacled men make lengthy (and irredeemably melancholy) commentary on issues of no interest whatsoever. But lo, here is *The Irish Times,* way back in 1988, releasing its inner Joe Duffy in the shape of this wicked photograph. Just to prove that it wasn't in the least funny, the picture ran on a business page alongside the stocks and shares. It was accompanied by an extended report on that year's *Irish Times* debate, which proposed the highly serious motion "That Trade Unions Are Becoming Increasingly Irrelevant". Among those speaking in favour of this proposal were the engineer and scientist Noel Mulcahy and the political economist Moore McDowell, both of whom opined - I'm summarising, but you get the drift - that trade unions had wrecked the economy and destroyed the lives of innocent consumers. Controversial, not to say contentious, stuff. The camera, however, has captured Mulcahy (left) and Moore (right) in a classic "Two Joe Duffys" moment. Two beardy men who have both - clearly - been to Specsavers. Two cheekily comic expressions. If not for the different hair partings, they might be twins. Or, at the very least, Zig and Zag. Or yin and yang. In real life, needless to say, Mulcahy and McDowell look nothing like each other. But look at one face in this photo and you find yourself looking in disbelief at the other, then back again, in a back-and-forth bounce that can only end by making you smile. And goodness knows we could all do with a smile. Maybe if we start with a smile, the Euro 2012 results - never mind the ongoing economic situation and all the rest of it - won't make us weep. **Published -02/06/2012**

Published June 20th, 1988
Photograph by Peter Thursfield

39

Behind the scenes

I have a cousin in Texas who adores JP Donleavy, and reckons *The Ginger Man* is a work of sublime genius. Outraged by my repeated shrugs of indifference and ignorance he sent me a copy of it recently, complete with foreword by Jay McInerney which declares the novel to be "one of the great stylistic tours de force of the 20th century". It is indeed an extraordinary piece of prose. For years, however, *The Ginger Man* was regarded in Ireland, much more prosaically, as the dirtiest book since Ulysses. First published in 1955, the tale of Sebastian Dangerfield - a young American living in Dublin with his English wife and baby daughter, and "studying law" at Trinity College, aka going on an almighty and prolonged bender - was promptly banned for obscenity. Donleavy's stage adaptation suffered a similar fate. After running for just three nights at the Gaiety Theatre, with Richard Harris in the role of Dangerfield, the play was withdrawn. This photograph captures the mood of the three principal actors in the *Ginger Man* drama as they peruse reports of the fracas in the newspapers. A dapper Donleavy, in the centre, looks more bemused than surprised. On the left, producer Philip Wiseman stares glumly at the camera. To the right of the frame the youthful Harris lounges on a sofa, his hair fashionably dishevelled. Where are they? Probably backstage at the Gaiety somewhere, in a room which could itself have come right out of *The Ginger Man*; net curtains which don't quite meet, lampshade askew, pipes on the wall exposed (but not in a good way). The accompanying report reads like a script for a mystery story. "Somebody" suggested to the Gaiety that cuts should be made to the production. The suggestion was declined by the company, which had signed a contract with the author forbidding any changes. The cutglass politeness is more bizarre than anything Sebastian Dangerfield at his most inebriated could dream up. The shadowy "somebody", no prizes for guessing, may well have been Archbishop John Charles McQuaid. Back in the 21st century, Johnny Depp is a big fan of The Ginger Man and is keen to bring it to the big screen. A happy ending at last? No pressure, JD and JP, but you guys could make my cousin Arthur a very happy man. **Published -02/06/2012**

Published June 20th, 1988
Photograph by Peter Thursfield

41

Merchant's arch

It was A quiet news day. The lead story on the front page of *The Irish Times* was devoted to sirloin steak, selling for eight shillings a pound, where a mere 12 months earlier it could be had for six - tops. "Over the past year the housewife has tried to offset the higher beef prices by eating more mutton and pork," the report explained. Clearly, in 1965, vegetarianism was not an option. Elsewhere on the front page, 23 people have been invited to become shareholders at the Abbey Theatre. And there are worries that Queen's University, Belfast might - might! - disaffiliate itself from the Union of Students in Ireland. Every cloud has a silver lining. Perhaps if war had broken out in West Cork, or a tsunami had engulfed Leitrim in the night, readers would not have been treated to this tranquil study by an unknown photographer. It's captioned "Sun and shadows at Merchant's Arch, Dublin". And a low, January sun at that, lighting the stones on the wall on the left to a gleaming brightness while casting lengthy shadows in front of the two main protagonists in the picture, a woman wrapped in winter coat and boots and a nun in full head-to-toe rig-out, including wimple. The narrow alleyway of Merchant's Arch runs alongside Merchant's Hall, built in 1821 as a meeting house for the Guild of Merchant Tailors. Within 20 years, this medieval organisation was disbanded: in 1841 the Municipal Reform Act set up the elected body which would be known as Dublin Corporation. From 1908 until the 1980s, Merchant's Hall housed a poplin and shirt factory. A watercolour of the arch by the painter William Orpen, at the National Gallery of Ireland, shows the alley festooned with loaded washing lines. Was the photographer just passing through, on his way to somewhere else, when he spotted this enigmatic pair? Or did he wait for the light and the composition to be just right? Where, come to think of it, were the women heading? We'll never know. Nowadays - if the number of images which turn up online is an accurate indication - the arch has to be one of the most photographed locations in Dublin. It may even appear on the front page of this newspaper on a quiet news day 50 years from now.

Published - 16/06/2012

Published: January 13th, 1965

Snakes alive!

Some pictures are worth a thousand words. Others make words outlandishly redundant. In the case of this glorious study of our famously slippery former Taoiseach wielding a snake - well, hey. What can we say? In July 1994, of course, Bertie Ahern was merely a Minister for Finance. It was in this capacity that he turned up to open the newly- refurbished Reptile House at Dublin Zoo. The first of the zoo's enclosures, Joe Carroll's wry front-page article reports, to be revamped in a style more closely resembling the natural habitat of the creatures destined to slither therein. "It will be a good place to study our animal friends and for them to study us as well," Bertie declared, blissfully unaware of just how ironically his words, not to mention his actions, would strike newspaper readers a mere 20 years into the future. As he approached the snake the Minister was heard to ask, "Does he bite?" (Pythons, Carroll observed tartly, don't bite; "they only wrap themselves around you for tenderising before you are swallowed whole.") But hang on a second. Aren't we being just little unfair? Isn't there another side to this story? The photographer may have captured Bertie in full-on laughing mode, but it's obvious from the story that he's uneasy about getting up close and personal with large reptiles. The expression on the face of his 12-year-old daughter Cecelia is revelatory. She, too, is smiling, but it's the taut smile of anxiety. Careful, there, Dad. Perhaps she added, in her own head, PS: I Love You. Anyhow, before we praise Bertie's bravery too much, we should read the final paragraph of the story. As ever with Irish politics, all is not quite as it seems. The snake in the photo is not a Reptile House resident. He is, in fact, Monty, "a house-trained, placid Burmese python who resides on the southside with a loving owner". He was borrowed "to make sure Bertie was not devoured by the two man-eating East African rock pythons who are on the way to the new Reptile House, thus causing a cabinet reshuffle." As for the snakes in the grass at the time, well, it now seems they weren't all living in the Reptile House either. **Published - 23/06/2012**

Published: July 30th, 1994
Photograph by Frank Miller

Portrush

The past two decades have been something of a rollercoaster for Portrush and Portstewart on the north Antrim coast. "The last resorts", as the headline on an *Irish Times* feature from 20 years ago put it, "before Iceland". Changing holiday preferences and political uncertainties have conspired to challenge these neighbouring resorts, which - like many traditional seaside towns all around Ireland's coastline - have been fighting against a long and vertiginous slide into shabbiness and neglect. *Irish Times* writer Robert O'Byrne was certainly not impressed by Portrush when he visited in the summer of 1991. The town's noisy streets, he observed, were "packed at weekends with some of Northern Ireland's most enthusiastic chip-eaters" and its "fine old neo-Tudor railway station" had been turned into a nightclub called "Tracks". He was less disapproving of next-door Portstewart, whose two miles of golden strand "oozes genteel respectability". The folks pictured on this fairground ride in Portrush are taking an altogether more cheerful view. They appear, in fact, to be having a whale of a time. The squeals of the girls in the front row are clearly audible. In the row behind, Dad sits with arms folded while Mum's hands are raised - either on the way to cover her eyes, or to make a grab for her daughters. Some passengers clutch their restraining straps in delight. Others gaze at the ground, wishing - perhaps - that they'd never left it. The daredevils in the back row are in seventh heaven. And why wouldn't they be? Portrush - from the Irish Port Rois, meaning "promontory port" - is spectacularly located on a mile-long peninsula which extends northwards into the Atlantic, offering panoramic views of the Causeway Coast, the hills of Donegal and even, on a fine day, Scotland. This would be a good summer to get out, belt up and give our custom to Ireland's hard-pressed coastal resorts. Seventh heaven awaits. And if that's not reason enough to get yourself to Portrush, how about the Irish Open Golf Championship, going on up there this very weekend? Posh enough for you? **Published -30/06/2012**

Published: July 3rd, 1991
Photograph by Peter Thursfield

47

48

Science superstars

We all know who this is - don't we? Oh, yes. No prizes for guessing the identity of the man in the middle in this photograph. It is, of course, Stephen Hawking, physicist extraordinaire and one of the most recognisable icons of our scientific times, pictured at a symposium in Dublin in the autumn of 1983. But can you name the smiling bespectacled man on the right? Ho hum. To my shame, I couldn't either. Clue: he was the first person to split the atom, thus confirming Einstein's famous equation $E = MC^2$. Another clue: he was born in Dungarvan, Co Waterford. Third clue: he won the Nobel Prize for Physics in 1951, for "pioneer work on the transmutation of atomic nuclei by artificially accelerated atomic particles". If you haven't recognised Ernest Walton by now, take a good look. He's one of our own and, despite his unassuming manner and genial smile, one of our all-time science greats. The man on the left is Lochlainn O'Raifeartaigh of the Dublin Institute of Advanced Studies, who has a theorem named after him and was no slouch on the supersymmetry front, either. Both of these Irish scientists are now dead, but that doesn't stop us from adding them - starting with Walton, who really does merit superstar status; after all, Prof Hawking hasn't won a Nobel Prize yet, has he? - to the icon pantheon. We're having a great science year. Another symposium is getting under way in Dublin this month, and not just any old symposium but Europe's largest science conference, the Euroscience Open Forum. With all the advance hoo-hah we're already learning lots about the current state of scientific endeavours worldwide. As the month goes on we will learn more. Some of it is difficult and some of it is easy. Learning to recognise Ernest Walton is a doddle. Unassuming manner. Genial smile. Spectacles. I'm doing it now. Spot the superstar scientist. You can join me if you like. **Published -07/07/2012**

Published October 8th, 1983
Photograph by Peter Thursfield

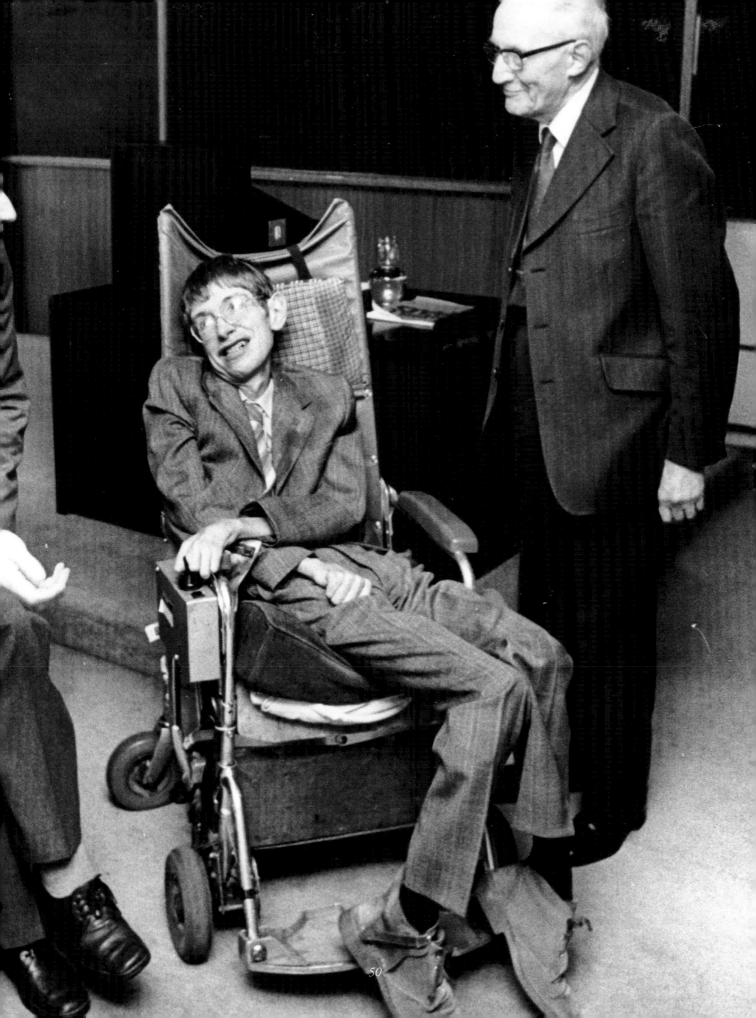

Shiver sisters

This delightful shot was captured by our eagle-eyed photographer Alan Betson at a Bread and Roses pageant on Grangegorman Road, Dublin, in the autumn of 1993. It was, to judge by the attire of the child who can (just) be seen in the right of the photograph, winter-coat weather. It was probably a bit on the chilly side for ankle socks and short dresses. Fine while you're doing whatever it is you do during the parade: not great while you're hanging around before and after. Which is why 10-year-old Suzanne Parks offered tiny tot Kelly McLoughlin, just four years old, a go of her anorak. Or more likely - look at the length of the sleeves and the size of the pockets - her mammy's anorak. At first glance they look like sisters, but that's probably just the hair-dos. Of course they may be related in some other way. They are, however, sisters in the best sense of the word, supporting each other in their time of need. Rose Schneiderman would surely approve. A Russian Jew who migrated to the US with her family in the 1890s, she became a prominent trade unionist, socialist and feminist. It was Schneiderman who coined the phrase "bread and roses" in a famous speech about the rights of working women - "the right to life as the rich woman has the right to life, and the sun and music and art ... the worker must have bread, but she must have roses, too" - which was later worked into a kitschy poem and, later still, into an even kitschier John Denver song. The spirit of the picture, though, sings out sure and true. It's funny because at first glance it looks as if the younger girl is just a disembodied head - and a head with a comically doleful expression, at that. It's moving because those coloured tights are just beginning to wrinkle at the knees. But the hug never wavers. Someone to hug you when you're freezing and your tights are letting you down. This photograph is a song, already. **Published - 14/07/2012**

Published October 26th, 1993
Photograph by Alan Betson

52

High-flying bulls

Never , they say, work with children or animals. They'll upstage you every time. The gentleman in the picture is a prize-winning Charolais bull by the wonderful name of Farmleigh Rebel. And the two-legged carbon-based life-forms on either side are, on the right, his keeper and stockman Louis O'Rafferty and, on the left, Benjamin Guinness, the third Earl of Iveagh, otherwise known as Viscount Elveden. The picture is a study in facial expressions. Farmleigh Rebel has good reason to look smug. He has just beaten all the other bulls at the Irish Charolais Cattle Society show and sale at Goffs, Co Kildare, into a cocked hat by taking both the Bunker Hunt trophy and the Champion Bull of Show awards. Mr O'Rafferty has the look of a man who knows all too well that Farmleigh Rebel might suddenly lurch to his right and give his aristocratic owner a hefty puck in the ribs. He is, therefore, poised to take any remedial action which might be necessary. Viscount Elveden, meanwhile, looks - well - hunted. Maybe he's standing in something unmentionable. Maybe he knows, deep down, that he's no match for this magnificent blue-blooded curly-headed creature whose forebears can - according to the Irish Charolais Cattle Society's excellent website - be traced back to east central France in the 14th century. Or maybe he's just not feeling terribly well; he was to die, of cancer, at the age of 55, just over a decade after this picture was taken. Farmleigh Rebel, for his part, made a suitably upper-crust 2,000 guineas and doubtless went on to sire many further editions of curly white critturs. First imported to Ireland in 1964, Charolais cattle were initially housed in an offshore quarantine station on Spike Island. The first public auction, at Maynooth Mart in 1969, saw a bull sell for 1,100 guineas. The bulls haven't gotten any bigger in the interim, but the prices have. In May this year another champion, Carrowkeel Graham, bred by Thomas Gormley from Elphin, Co Roscommon, was sold for €6,100. Pigs may not be able to fly; Charolais bulls, apparently, can soar quite nicely. **Published -21/07/2012**

Published September 18th, 1981
Photograph by Pat Langan

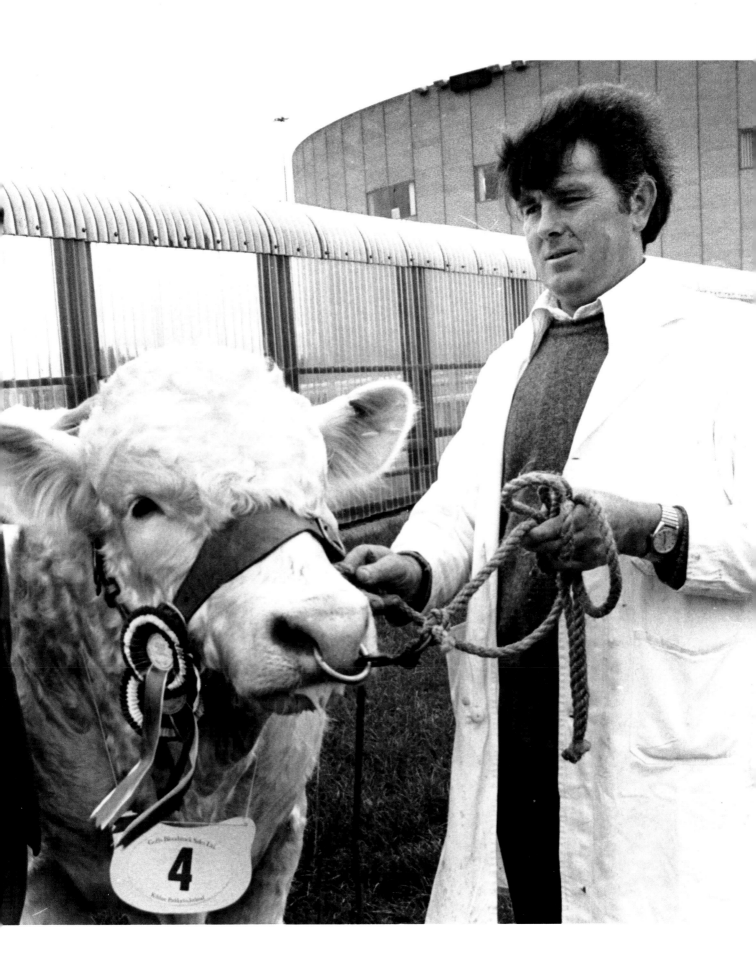

Full-on Frankie

Conspirators in some rakish spy movie from turn-of-the-20th-century Vienna? Attendees at a top-notch cocktail party? No. The picture shows, of all things, the launch of a new PR company. Frankie Byrne Public Relations Ltd was the brainchild of the woman who would later become famous - infamous, even - in Ireland as the radio agony aunt "Dear Frankie". In 1963, however, she was leaving the McConnells PR agency to set up on her own - prompting her former boss, John McConnell, to present her with a new office desk and wish her well. Ah, the innocence of public relations past. Frankie was determined to start with a stylish splash. Hence this classy bash at Jury's Hotel in Dublin, attended by the Lord Mayor of Dublin Alderman JJ O'Keeffe TD, and 200 guests. Her outfit is as immaculate as you'd expect from the first woman to set up a PR company in Ireland: small wonder that she was hired to cover the visit of the über-glam US president JFK to Ireland later that year. Flanking their new PR guru in our photograph - and no slouches on the style front themselves, it must be said - are high-profile clients (left) Mr C Gordon Lambert, sales director of Jacob's biscuits, and (right) Mr James A Chapman of Switzer's department store on Grafton Street. In the centre, Frankie's enigmatic smile and ever-so-slightly-raised eyebrows seem to say: "Well, boys, I got you into the paper on day one. Pretty good going, huh?" It was Jacob's which would entice Frankie on to RTÉ radio as presenter of a domestic science slot on one of the company's sponsored shows. Not being the domestic goddess type, she quickly suggested an agony aunt slot instead - and a legend was born. In later life, the going got tough for Frankie Byrne as she turned to drink and prescription drugs. She got clean, dropped out of the public eye, was diagnosed with Alzheimer's. She died in 1993. But as the ongoing success of Niamh Gleeson's play *Dear Frankie* proves, she's still remembered with great affection. Audience reaction to the play has even inspired an RTÉ radio documentary - a full circle with which this full-on character would, surely, be delighted **Published -28/07/2012**

Published January 29th, 1963
Photograph by Jimmy McCormack

A good judge of character

Irish summers. don't you just love them? Rain and more rain. Wellies and brollies. Sodden festival-goers in muddy fields. Once you get indoors and get dry again, though, it's the characters you remember, rather than the weather - especially when you peer back, through photographs, into summers past. The Dublin Horse Show has had its fair share of characters over the years. Take this one, decanted on to a shooting stick at an improbably jaunty angle, bowler hat in hand, pipe in mouth, a broad smile on his aquiline face and his left hand raised in . . . what? The thumb-and-first-finger circle that denotes "perfection"? All the better for whoever or whatever he's judging if that's the case - though he may, of course, just have an eyelash in his eye. Come to think of it, he has something in his eye all right: a glint that suggests a zest for life. It fairly zooms out of the picture. To be fair, the fact that the sun is shining helps the mood. As does the photographer's skill in capturing the play of light on that weather-beaten face. The judge's formal attire harks back to another era. There was a time when showjumping was an all-male affair - ladies were not allowed to enter "leaping" competitions at the RDS until 1919 - as well as the preoccupation of a privileged social class. These days, everyone is welcome at the show - which this year starts a week later than usual on August 15th - with a plethora of family activities going on around and between the equine events which are still at its heart. Even the word "judging" has taken on a much wider meaning, with the RDS student art awards and the National Craft Competition becoming part of the mix. As to whether this year's show will produce a Dublin character for summers future to remember with fondness, well, we'll just have to wait and see.

Published -04/08/2012

Published: August 3rd,1977
Photograph by Peter Thursfield

58

Coming up Roses

The Rose of Tralee festival really is an extraordinary institution. Love it or loathe it - and we've had all the finely honed feminist arguments for years, plus the priceless *Father Ted* parody, the "Lovely Girls" competition - it's as vibrant as ever in 2012, shaping up to get going for the umpteenth year in a row. Our photograph shows a bunch of Roses from 1986, heading to strut their stuff upon the Kerry stage. Somewhere among those faces is the 1986 winner, Noreen Cassidy, aka the Leeds Rose, who went on to become chief executive of the festival and chief executive of the RTÉ People in Need Trust telethon before settling in Galway to run a marquee and event management company with her partner. No wilting violet she, even the staunchest feminist would have to agree. Indeed, whatever one's feelings about the competition - my own, I confess, being that the whole idea of "judging" women in this manner is anachronistic, if not outright creepy - there's no faulting the Roses themselves. Cassidy's predecessor, the 1985 Chicago Rose, Michele McCormack, went on to win an Edward R Murrow award as a broadcast journalist. Roses have blossomed into successful actors and blazed brightly on the stock exchange. I happen to know a Rose from a decade ago. She has two lovely girls of her own now, and is a regular young working mother, just trying to get by in the urban jungle that is contemporary Dublin. So let's hear it for the Roses. Maybe one of these days, we'll find a more adult way of celebrating the wild and wonderful women of Ireland - and of the world. Meanwhile, even such hardy geraniums as the Rose of Tralee festival do change and evolve. In 1986 the festival was officially opened by Charles J Haughey, who recited a poem composed for the occasion. This year the competition will kick off with a gig by Jedward. Now that's progress. Isn't it?
Published -11/08/2012

Published: August 3rd,1977
Photograph by Pat Langan

60

Unholy Moses

Thou shalt not kill. Thou shalt not steal. Thou shalt not stick out thy tongue at thy mother and father . . . In April 1958, Dubliners were treated to Charlton Heston's performance as Moses when Cecil B De Mille's big-screen epic *The Ten Commandments* was screened at the Ambassador cinema. Even now, De Mille's shots of Heston posed against a sky riven by lightning, arms raised and beard flying, define our notion of what a proper Old Testament prophet ought to look like. After the Dublin showing of the movie, the Hestons turned up at a press reception at the Gresham Hotel, which is where our photograph was taken - though the photographer's name has not been recorded. Heston pere looks as if he has been freshly chiselled from thoroughbred rocks. His wife, Lydia, is elegant in draped jersey and pearls. But it's young Fraser Heston who steals the show in this image. Three years old, cute as a button, and clearly no saint - despite having played the infant Moses in De Mille's biblical extravaganza at the age of just three months - he is obviously at home in front of a phalanx of cameras, well able to face down what the writer of *An Irishman's Diary*, who attended the press reception, described as "the largest gathering of newspapermen" Heston had encountered outside the US. Heston went on to become a Hollywood legend, not just for such classic movies as *Planet of the Apes* and *Ben-Hur*, but, in later life, for his conservative politics and, in particular, his outspoken support for the National Rifle Association. Fraser Heston would go on to direct a number of movies, including his father in a 1990 version of *Treasure Island*. Back in April 1958, the Hestons have the look of the model American family. Nevertheless *The Irish Times* did not publish this photograph. Perhaps - cute as he seems to us - Fraser Heston was just too far from the model of a 1950s Irish child. The ones who were told, "Thou shalt keep a low profile if thou knowest what is good for thee". **Published -18/08/2012**

Published April, 1958

61

What a bargain

It's that Mexican sombrero that does it. There was a pretty grim caption to accompany this photograph, to the effect that north Dublin farmers were being forced to sell their vegetables at the side of the road "at a price which leaves no room for profit". These days, of course, we're used to seeing Wexford spuds for sale on the roadside and direct selling from farmer to customer, especially when the word "organic" is involved, is a plus for all sides. In 1977, though, the idea was considered outlandish. Maybe that explains the distinctly Wild West flavour of this image, which seems to contain an entire reel of dramatic narrative. The sombrero'ed kid standing on the back of a pick-up in pouty gunslinger pose like an extra from *Three Amigos*. The telegraph poles at unruly angles are like cacti in the desert. The man standing watchfully towards the rear, arms behind his back, his expression unreadable. The boy lugging the bag toward the camera, his angelic curls offset by the strain of his distinctly earthbound job. And then the fair-haired woman stepping forward to offer money, as if she was approaching the checkout in a supermarket. She strikes an incongruous note, as if she had strayed into the scene from another movie altogether. As for the spuds themselves, well, in 1977, £1 for a big bag was a bargain. This very month a kerfuffle over pricy potatoes has broken out on the website donegaldaily. com, where a reader reported shelling out €5 for a 7lb bag on a road out of Letterkenny. The tubers were reportedly delicious, but were they, a witty follow-up post wanted to know, Kerr's Pinks or Records? Spud-related puns aside, there is a serious side to it all. Talk of potential potato shortages has an emotional resonance in Ireland that it might not have elsewhere. Whatever happens with this year's crop, we're not going to starve the way people did in the 1840s. But if rain continues to decimate our soggy fields and farms, the chips may be down - and the prices up - for the foreseeable future.
Published -August 23rd, 1977

Published: August 3rd, 1977

POTATOES
£1 PER
BAG

Uncertain prospects

It was a *Dazzling Prospect* right enough: a new play from the popular Irish writer Molly Keane, with two of the best-known names in the British entertainment business among the cast. But this publicity shot, taken at Dublin's Olympia Theatre in the spring of 1961, somehow suggests, not a Dazzling Prospect, but a Dodgy Proposition. Keane, in the centre of the picture, looks frail and pale. To the left of the frame Margaret Rutherford stares sleepily at the camera, looking as if she's about to doze off at any moment. Sir John Gielgud, flanked by the play's co-author, John Perry (left), and director, Richard Leech (right), clutches a glass of something far too small - which may explain why he appears to be on the point of running away. Leech offers a manic baring of teeth. Only Perry, hand on hip, appears halfway normal. In fairness, Rutherford - darling of many a big-screen classic comedy caper in the company of Norman Wisdom, Donald Sinden and Peter Sellers - always looks pretty much the same, whether she's cycling around the Kent countryside in Blithe Spirit, cape billowing behind her, or sleuthing as Miss Marple, which is how we mostly remember her today. What people who tune in to reruns of those early Marples on satellite TV probably don't know is that Rutherford had a life so extraordinary that even Agatha Christie wouldn't have dared put it into fictional form. Her father - William Benn, whose brother John was Tony Benn's grandfather - murdered her grandfather. Young Margaret took her mother's name and was brought up by an aunt. To carve a hugely successful stage and screen career out of such inauspicious beginnings - and with such unpromising looks into the bargain - was a remarkable achievement. Although it moved from the Olympia to London for a run at the Globe Theatre, *Dazzling Prospect* wasn't Rutherford's finest hour. Our rather glum photograph proved prescient; critics gave the play such a savaging that Keane didn't write another word for decades. Rutherford kept working for another six years. She was diagnosed with Alzheimer's disease and died in 1972, aged 80. **Published -01/09/2012**

Published April 24th, 1961
Photograph by Dermot Barry

All the young dudes

As another school year swings into top gear under a cloud of economic doom and gloom, it's hard not to feel for a generation which is trying to knuckle down to studies of one sort or another. The bigger 21st-century picture can be a daunting thing. All you have to do to offset such gloomy thoughts, however, is get up close and personal with a school. Any school. If you're signing up for an evening class, take a look at the walls and corridors around you: chances are they're covered in posters, paintings and notices which exude an almost palpable energy, creativity and optimism. All of which - and more - emanates from this photograph of the winners of the 1987 All-Ireland Management Competition for schools. The team of young hotshots from St Benildus College, Kilmacud, Co Dublin includes (from left) Damian Lawlor, Ross Mayne, Garret O'Neill, Fearghal O'Boyle (captain), Fergal Byrne and Adrian Crean. The suits, the haircuts, the rowdy horseplay, the raw confidence, the well-manicured teeth: all there in spades as the lads celebrate their victory. This, folks, was at the end of the 1980s, now infamous as the most miserable time in living Irish memory. It was, as a close examination of the coiffures in this photograph proves, the era of the dodgy fringe. Where are they now, our half-dozen management wannabes? Thanks to the wonder that is the internet we can reveal that Ross Mayne is chief executive of a Leopardstown company called Munich Re Automated Solutions Ltd, part of the international German Munich Re group. And Adrian Crean is the managing director of McDonald's Ireland - the first Irish person who has held that exalted position, we are told. Pretty good going for guys who emerged from secondary school at the end of the awful 1980s. They didn't know what lay ahead of them, any more than we do now - but according to Mayne they were inspired by a "fantastic" teacher by the name of Frank Scott, now retired. We hope things turned out well for the other members of the group. In any case, take heart, all ye who pack your schoolbags this weekend. **Published -08/09/2012**

Published February 26th, 1987
Photograph by Dermot Barry

Keep on trucking

We may fondly imagine 2012 was a bad summer - glorious September weather notwithstanding - but it was nothing compared to the annus horribilis that was the summer of 1981. Hunger strikers were dying in the North, there was rioting on the Merrion Road, Dublin following a H-Block protest and the coalition government was facing a Dáil vote on a tough supplementary Budget which threatened to bring the whole shaky edifice crashing down. On top of which, a "CIE craftsmen's strike" decimated bus services in Dublin, Cork and Galway. Happily for hard-pressed Dublin commuters the Army was swiftly drafted in, with 50 trucks running from seven points around the city centre to and from the suburbs. This military mercy operation involved 240 privates and 17 officers. It took commuters a while to get the hang of it - no texting, no tweeting, no electronic signs at bus stops - but once they did, the truck dubbed the "Tallaght Express" did particularly brisk business. Each truck held 30 people on hard chairs which may explain why the folks in our photo look a bit stiff and sore as they clamber down from the back of the lorry. The woman in front swinging a sports bag in her right hand appears to be squinting in the sunshine, so presumably reading lights were not available inside. Another woman is approaching the stepladder with all the enthusiasm of a swimmer dipping a toe into the Arctic. She is watched by a soldier who really, you might think, ought to be giving her a helping hand. As to the soldier in the foreground, well, he's either executing some sort of exotic peace-time goose-step or trying to pull up his socks without disturbing his highly polished boots. Some commuters expressed unease at the service on the grounds that it was, technically speaking, strike-breaking. But most were delighted with it. "It's just as comfortable as CIE," one Clondalkin-bound man told an *Irish Times* reporter. "And it's much more regular."

Published -15/09/2012

Published July 21st, 1981
Photograph by Jimmy McCormack

70

Sister act

Smile. click. And the happy faces of nine women are captured on celluloid. The hairstyles and accessories - look at those immaculate rows of pearls - indicate that we're in the 1950s. As for the eyes, you don't have to study them for very long before you realise that these ladies are all members of one family. They are, in fact, the Larkin sisters from South Circular Road in Dublin: (back row, from left) Carmel (17), Sheila (25), May (28); (middle row) Philomena (18), Monica (19); (front row) Veronica (11), Catherine (27), Theresa (23) and Angela (8). Why were the lovely Larkins photographed for the *Times Pictorial* magazine? Strange, but true: on February 12th, 1955, the newspaper published a picture of nine Larkin sisters from Letterkenny, Co Donegal, along with a breezy caption that asked whether any other Irish household could "beat this record of nine attractive girls in the one family". A couple of days later the people at *Times Pictorial* got a call from a Dublin man. "It's a bit of a coincidence, really," he said. "I have nine daughters and four sons, too. Exactly the same family as the Larkins of Donegal." Quite a coincidence, agreed the folks from *Times Pictorial*. "And my name is Larkin," said the caller. Wow, said the *TP* - or words to that effect. A photographer was despatched to South Circular Road forthwith. Imagine the bustle and merriment that must have gone on as they all got into position. *Times Pictorial* published a slightly different shot, a landscape, but we like this portrait-shaped picture. Still as it is, monochrome as it is, it portrays nine colourful characters in almost 3D action: a waterfall of Larkins. Apart from the two youngest, who are more guarded than amused - suggesting that whatever has been said to make everyone else laugh may have gone over their innocent young heads - every single Dublin Larkin is bubbling over with mischief. The Letterkenny Larkins, by the way, looked equally stylish - if a little more serious - in their photo. What the male Larkins looked like, meanwhile, went unrecorded. The two families are not related. **Published -22/09/2012**

Published February 1955

72

Paws for thought

We tend to think that China didn't figure on our cultural radar in the days before Asian fusion takeaways and the large-scale manufacture, in Chinese cities, of everything from iPads to plastic bath toys. Yet here, in February 1970, is Chairman Mao beaming benevolently from the window of Progressive Books and Periodicals on Dublin's Essex Street, while some passers-by are clearly riveted by the display of material available for purchase. Well, not quite. The dog - though he does have one ear cocked in the direction of the bookshop window - isn't riveted at all. On the contrary, is there something about the squareness of his stance which is just the teeniest bit disapproving? Maybe, in 1970, even the dogs in the street could tell that the Communist Party of Ireland (Marxist-Leninist) was beginning to drift away from its staunch support for the chairman. Come the Sino-Albanian split of 1978, the party would side with Enver Hoxha's Albanian brand of Communism. Or maybe he's just patiently waiting for his owner to get back to walking the walk. Are the man and woman in the photograph a couple, or two passing strangers? There's no way to tell, although the fact that the woman is sporting a headscarf suggests she harks back to an older generation. Her boots, her bag, even the way the hem of her coat hangs - she could be an extra in a spy movie set in eastern Europe. The way the books are displayed in the bookshop window, ranked in slightly dismal rows, adds to the effect. The fact that the people are both leaning slightly to the right is probably more accidental than ideological. The CPI (Marxist-Leninist) also ran bookshops, at various times, in Limerick and Cork. Its finest hour was probably when David Vipond, a research chemist from Trinity College Dublin, stood at a byelection in Monaghan. He got just 157 first preferences - clearly the Monaghan Maoists were slacking when it came to winning hearts and minds - but he caused quite a stir which, briefly, brought the party on to the mainstream radar. It disbanded in 2003. **Published -29/09/2012**

Published: February 20th, 1970

Great gourd almighty

A bit heavy on the pallet? That's for sure. This hefty 480lb pumpkin was spotted by our eagle-eyed photographer as it was being unloaded on South Anne Street in Dublin. Despite the background sign which reads "sub rolls" and "sandwiches", however, the giant gourd was never destined to end up in anybody's bowl of soup. Instead, it was headed to a nearby gardening shop, where it was put on display in order to persuade customers of the effectiveness of a fertiliser which, by 1991, had produced 50 world records and 19 entries in the Guinness Book of Records. Not that the passersby in the photograph appears to be particularly impressed - they're not even stopping to watch as the delivery man measures up to the phenomenal fruit. The super-squash in our "Mr Pumpkin-Head" photo is, it must be said, a mere sprat compared to the record-breakers of today. A maple farmer from Ontario, Canada, by the name of Jim Bryson has been growing these behemoths for years - and having achieved a whopping 1,818lb specimen in 2011, is determined to achieve the first one-tonne pumpkin in history before he bows out of the game. (That's 2,000lbs to you and me.) I'm guessing most of us will be happy to settle for more modestly-sized pumpkins when Hallowe'en comes around at the end of this month. Although a more authentically Irish option would actually be a turnip - a much tougher proposition which, in days of yore, our ancestors carved, lit from inside and left on the doorstep on All Hallows' Eve to ward off evil spirits. And here was me thinking it was a feat of strength and skill to get one into a pot of winter vegetable soup ... **Published -06/10/2012**

Published October 26th, 1991
Photograph by Peter Thursfield

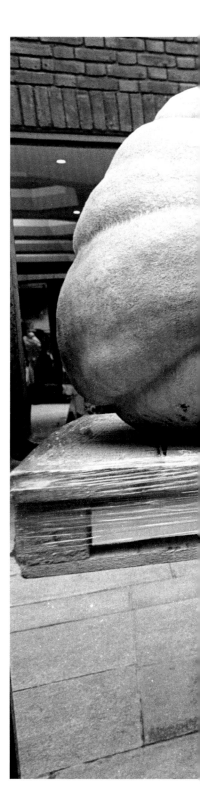

75

Sub Rolls   Sandwiches

85-D-3741

The oldest wringer in town

No prizes for spotting Sonny Knowles, showband singer and man about town, dressed as his trademark debonair self in a smart suit and shoes shiny enough to pick up signals from deep space. But why, rather than a microphone, is he brandishing what looks like an oversized saucepan lid - and peering into an ancient top-loader washing machine as if in search of missing prehistoric socks? Well - and we promise we're not making this up - the photograph shows the prizewinners in the Oldest Servis Washing Machine in Ireland competition. On the left is Margaret Sweeney from Co Sligo. The woman standing next to her is Phil Sexton, from Co Cork. "The oldest wringer in town," proclaims our clever caption-writer. It's clear that the joke is aimed, not just at the winning machine - purchased by one Elizabeth McArdle from Dundalk, in 1949, for goodness' sake, making it almost worthy of inclusion in a collection of historical household appliances at the National Museum of Ireland - but at the bould Sonny, who, over a 60-year career, was always as likely to tell a joke against himself as he was to burst into song. He is still fondly remembered by many for his double entry in the 1966 Irish National Song Contest, scoring nul points with The *Menace from Ennis* and *Chuaigh Mé Suas Don Chluiche Mór*, and finishing - triumphantly - in equal 10th place with himself. Despite two battles with cancer, he's still singing, taking to the stage for occasional fundraisers, such as the concert he did recently to help raise money to buy new instruments for the Tallaght Youth Band. Never mind the washing machine: this man deserves a prize in his own right. He'll be 80 next month. Happy birthday, Sonny Knowles. **Published -20/10/2012**

Published: December 11th, 1990
Photograph by Matt Kavanagh

Pitch perfect

If you've ever bought a copy of *The Irish Times* from the vendors outside Dunnes Stores in Cornelscourt, who always offer a smile whatever the weather conditions, you'll appreciate this story. Some readers may even remember Tom Prior, who sold newspapers at the corner of Leeson Street and Earlsfort Terrace for more than 50 years. This shot, which marked his decision to retire at the age of 71, shows a man unbowed by years of standing in the cold. His expression is dreamy - maybe daydreaming helped pass the time - but his back is straight and his shoulders are square. Clearly, standing outdoors six days a week from 1921 to 1978 didn't do his spirit any harm. He was, however - as he told our reporter, Ella Shanahan - slightly peeved on the day in May 1947 when he braved an unseasonal snowstorm to bring the latest news to his customers. When he totted up his totals after this bizarre meteorological experience, he discovered he was short one shilling which meant he had not earned so much as a cent from his shivery stint. Most days, though, Prior began at 5.50am when he would collect part of his newspaper load from the GPO on O'Connell Street. Those papers were for delivery to Hatch Street, Adelaide Road, Harcourt Terrace and surrounding streets. After that, he went to his spot on the corner of St Stephen's Green to await the delivery of the rest of his papers, where he stayed until 10.30 am. Come the publication of the evening papers, he took up another position to sell those as well. It was, he told *The Irish Times*, a hard life; "but he liked it - and he made a good living". Though not good enough, clearly, to allow him to retire early. **Published -27/10/2012**

Published: April 7th, 1978
Photograph by Eddie Kelly

Showing fortitude

Some statues look statuesque, and others look . . . well, just the teeniest bit silly. When you see him from ground level the statue of Fortitude at Dublin Castle strikes a heroic pose, spear at the ready in his right arm. Up close, as our photograph shows, he has a pot belly and a Monty Python moustache. And as our photographer knew perfectly well, minus its spear that raised right arm is endearingly effete, suggesting that Fortitude is about to dance off into the sunset. The impression of almost pantomime absurdity is heightened by the statue's feathery helmet - and the goofy expression on the face of the lion cub in the bottom right-hand corner of the image. This cat isn't threatening evil-doers with its roar. It's giving its owner's hairy knee an affectionate puck with its oversized head. The picture was taken in the summer of 1988 when Fortitude and his "twin" sister, Justice, were being replaced on either side of the castle's Bedford Tower after a two-year restoration programme. Looking thoughtful at Fortitude's side - looking, come to think of it, the image of masculinity, bearded, hard-hatted and blue-collared - is the statue restorer Russel Turner. He definitely doesn't look as though he's about to accept the statue's invitation to the waltz. Perhaps he's just relieved to get the statues back into place without losing any limbs - either his or theirs. Fortitude and Justice are among Ireland's oldest public sculptures. They were made in 1753 by John Van Nost the Younger, the wonderfully named nephew of a Flemish sculptor who had moved to Dublin three years earlier. The statues are almost as old as Handel's *Messiah*, first performed in Dublin in 1742. Which means that Fortitude has stood his ground for more than 250 years, gazing out over our capital city as it goes about its daily business. No wonder he looks ready to flee. But he never has. Not yet . . . **Published -03/11/2012**

Published: August 8th, 1988
Photograph by Peter Thursfield

Tapirazzi

We're all familiar with the paparazzi, but haven't these kids got hold of the wrong end of the lens? I mean, aren't they supposed to be focusing on the beautiful people? Still, though. Aaaww. Oblivious to its own homeliness, the tapir at the centre of this mini-photographic frenzy is shimmying along as confidently as any catwalk supermodel. It even appears to be smiling for the cameras. Earlier this year, there were more smiles at Dublin Zoo when a pair of Brazilian tapirs, Rio and Marmaduke, became the proud parents of a male calf. Being the child of a digital age, photos of this stripey sprog are all over the internet and it is, in truth, a cute kid - even for an unprepossessing odd-toed ungulate. The young snappers in our photo - Liam Hyland, Andrew Bowell and Brian Edge - were preparing for the 1989 Fuji Young Photographer of the Year Competition. Now head of product management at computer games software company Havok, Andrew Bowell remembers the occasion well. "It was a trip organised by the photography club in Wesley College, where I was a pupil," he says. "I was lucky enough to have inherited a hand-me-down 'real' camera from my brother. I always loved photography and also the idea of being able to develop prints yourself. I don't think I ever managed that last bit successfully but it was a cool idea all the same. "The idea of capturing images - and in particular, the way you felt at a particular place and time - always intrigued me." Interesting that Bowell went on to work in an area of technology which gives visual life to all sorts of ideas. Since he and some friends set up Havok 12 years ago, the company's products have helped create special effects in such movies as *The Matrix, Watchmen* and *Quantum of Solace.* The past two decades haven't, alas, given tapirs much to smile about. One of the world's top 10 endangered animals, their rainforest habitat in south America has been devastated by man-made industry - and of the four species still in existence, all are in catastrophic decline. Makes this tapir look a whole lot prettier, when you think about it.
Published -10/11/2012

Published February 6th, 1989
Photograph by Jack McManus

83

Going, going, gone

This edition of the magazine has probably given you all kinds of constructive ideas about downsizing, saving, living within your means and all the rest of it. But if all else fails, you may have to resort to the cash in the attic strategy. It does happen. People have unearthed priceless artworks in the most unexpected of places. It's not so long since Caravaggio's *Taking of Christ* turned up in a Jesuit diningroom; and a painting by Paul Henry, T*he Bog Road*, was "discovered" on the BBC's *Antiques Roadshow* programme two years ago. It was valued at €45,000. In the art world, of course, everything is relative. And in Ireland, massive prices being paid for paintings is a relatively recent phenomenon. Our photo captures what has been described as the moment the Irish art market exploded: the sale of Jack Butler Yeats's *Harvest Moon* at James Adam and Sons in September 1989. Out of the blue, the painting made a record price: it was bought by Michael Smurfit for £280,000. Maybe that's why the two young male assistants to auctioneer Brian Coyle appear so uniformly gobsmacked. The young woman on the right of the picture has her arms folded - is she just in shock, or having some subliminal premonition of the boom-and-bust to come? - while the auctioneer has his hand raised in what looks, from our sadder, wiser perspective, like a gesture of warning. But if you do find a long-lost Yeats in your attic, you may well be raising your arm in triumph - as a millionaire. *The Wild Ones* was sold in 1999 for €1,233,000. As recently as September last year, *A Fair Day, Mayo* also made a million at Adam's. And that Paul Henry landscape, valued on the *Antiques Roadshow* at €45,000, fetched a healthy €73,000. Now, what's that sticking out from behind the dodgy bargain-basement printer and the bag of too-tight jeans . . . ? **Published -24/11/2012**

Published: September 29th, 1989
Photograph by Paddy Whelan

The picture house

Once upon a time, cinemas were purpose-built, somewhere you had to go if you wanted to watch a movie. Most of these buildings have been reused or recycled now, including the Sutton Cinema in north Dublin, pictured here, which is now a branch of Superquinn. Our story from 1967 reports that the cinema was bought by Quinn's Supermarkets Ltd for £100,000. It had been in the movie business for 30 years. The transformation saw the building swell to more than double its size and provide ample parking spaces - a facility that wasn't high on the priority list in the heyday of the local picture house. When the photo was taken the cinema had just one week of life left to go, which may account for the slightly spooky mood it evokes. Or maybe it's the unhappy expression on the face of the elderly gentleman sitting on the grotty concrete bench, its side stained with who knows what. He is switching from one set of glasses to another, perhaps in an attempt to get some more acceptable-looking news from his paper. Next to him on the bench a woman gazes across the street, as if mesmerised by its eerie emptiness. The cars complete the surreal retro feel. This could be a still from a Stephen King movie - complete with ironic touches such as the 7Up delivery van on the far right and the "grocer" sign to the left (signs of things to come, obviously). Since the 1960s the Superquinn chain has had some dramas of its own though it is still with us, one of the few Irish supermarkets left on the scene. But supermarkets are changing too. Remember when they used to be places where you had to go if you wanted to buy essential household supplies such as food or toilet roll? Now - especially as Christmas looms - they're more like cinemas, places where people go at weekends for entertainment. Or in search of such household essentials as camping equipment and cordless drills.
Published -01/12/2012

Published September 9th, 1967
Photograph by Dermot Barry

Oh yes, I can boogie

It's time to polish up our velvety frocks and our party pieces. But however well we scrub up this festive season, we're unlikely to present as singular an appearance as this extraordinary lady. The occasion was a tea party, organised by the Red Cross and hosted by Denis Guiney and his wife Mary, the owners of Clery's department store just after Christmas in 1954. The guests were 120 pensioners, all single and - according to the caption - "most of them lonely". But not on this merry afternoon. Denis Guiney - on the right of the picture - appears to have enjoyed himself hugely as master of ceremonies for the day. The piano player, Jack Davies, offers a somewhat apprehensive smile to the camera as he prepares to accompany 84-year-old Mrs Leslie for her party piece. We're not told her first name, or what song she sang. Given the cheeky expression on her face and the amusement of the pianist, however, it may not have been exactly *Hark! the Herald Angels*. But she's shaping up in a delightfully professional manner, her hand resting on the back of the pianist's chair, her back straight, coat and hat firmly in place. They give her a regal look, those outdoor clothes: the coat with its mayoral swathe of fur around her shoulders, the hat at precisely the right angle above her glasses, her booted feet those of a tiny dancer. Guiney, meanwhile, sports a raincoat over his three-piece suit: even the hard-working pianist hasn't dared to strip to his shirt-sleeves. It wouldn't do for party attire in the bling-struck 21st century. Obviously the ambient indoor temperature, despite the merriment, was pretty chilly. And if you look closely at that Christmas tree you'll notice that it's pretty sparsely decorated compared to the groaning, laden trees of today. What goes around, mind you, has a nasty habit of coming around. Denis Guiney rescued Clery's from receivership a decade or so before our picture was taken. Since he and his wife Mary died, the shop has had a bit of a bumpy ride. Hopefully, it will still be with us in another half-century. The return of coats and hats at parties, however, we could probably live without.
Published -08/12/2012

Published January 9th, 1954
Photograph by Jack McManus

89

Ba da bing

You can scarcely switch on a radio or a television, or venture into a shop, these days without the danger of "I'm Dreamin' of a White Christmas . . ." suddenly drifting into your airspace. Bing Crosby's bendy golden drawl is all very well, but over the past decade this particular slice of it has been played and replayed so often that many of us are now, instead, dreaming of the sound of silence for the months of October and November, if not December. When Crosby first pulled That Song out of his Santa hat on Christmas Day 1941, few listeners to his NBC radio show, the Kraft Music Hour - sponsored, oddly enough, by a cheese company - could have suspected that it would one day be the biggest-selling single of all time, with estimated sales of 50 million copies worldwide. Nowadays, it is, pretty much, the only thing people know about Crosby. But as our photo shows, there was more to the American singer and actor than that lazy bass-baritone. He was a huge fan of thoroughbred horse racing, bought his first racehorse in 1935, and was a founding partner of the Del Mar Thoroughbred Club in California, one of whose stars was the legendary Seabiscuit. On this side of the Atlantic, Crosby won the Irish Derby in 1965 with the colt Meadow Court, which he co-owned, prompting him to regale the winners' circle at the Curragh with an impromptu rendition of *When Irish Eyes Are Smiling*. In the photo, there are more smiles as Crosby and trainer Paddy Prendergast, both in natty race attire, acknowledge the victory of Crosby's horse Dominion Day at the Blandford Stakes at the Curragh. The horse, for its part, looks worried. Indeed, it appears to be foaming at the mouth. Perhaps it fears a repeat performance of *When Irish Eyes Are Smiling*. Or worse: after all, it's nearly the end of August. Not too soon, surely, for a blast of *White Christmas*?

Published -15/12/2012

Published August 28th, 1967
Photograph by Dermot Barry

91

A true Dubliner

He has a Dickensian, ghost-of-Christmas-past look about him, this über-dapper gentleman with his crisp collar, his neatly-rolled umbrella, his gleaming leather gloves and those debonair waxed moustaches. Who is he? Most people probably won't recognise him. And yet the article which accompanied this photograph in the spring of 1954 begins: "If you woke a Dubliner in the middle of the night and asked him the name of the Lord Mayor, it is long odds that he would mutter, without opening his eyes; 'Alfie Byrne'." The piece celebrated the 72nd birthday of the man who had been elected Lord Mayor of Dublin a record 10 times between 1930 and 1955. To get to the beginning of Alfie Byrne's extraordinary story, however, you need to go back to 1882 - a mere dozen years, as it happens, after the death of Charles Dickens - when he was born, the son of a Dublin docker. He sold theatre programmes and worked in a pub before buying his own bar, The Vernon on Dublin's Talbot Street. He entered politics at the age of 27 and after a spell on Dublin Corporation was elected MP for Dublin Harbour in 1915. After the Treaty he was elected to Dáil Éireann as an Independent TD. For the majority of Dubliners, however, Alfie Byrne was a civic rather than a political institution. In his quasi-Victorian garb he was an instantly recognisable figure on the streets of the capital, famous for his habit of greeting everyone he met with a handshake - or, if he was on his bike, a wave of his hard hat. Our portrait is a more formal affair, a study in shades and textures of black which captures the razor-sharp pinstripe of the suit trousers, the soft wool of the overcoat, the well-worn leather of the gloves. The subject himself seems to materialise out of the darkness behind him; or perhaps he's about to fade into it, since he would die just two years after this picture was taken. He has not been forgotten by his native city, however. Many artefacts and documents associated with him can be seen at The Little Museum of Dublin on St Stephen's Green.

Published -22/12/2012

Published: March 23rd, 1954

93

Happy feet

Life is a difficult business. And when the chips are down - or the curtain is about to go up - we all react differently. Before it ever began, the year 1984 had a bad reputation thanks to George Orwell's dystopian novel. It predicted a world in which uncaring capitalist superstates jostle for power while an increasingly devastated populace is cowed by ubiquitous posters bearing the caption "Big Brother Is Watching You", and monitored - both in public and in private - by an instrument known as the telescreen. Well, thank goodness that never came to pass, eh? In real life 1984 turned out to be just another year, strewn with its fair share of random delights and disasters. One of the delights was the annual show given by the tiny dancers of the Irish National College of Dance at the Oscar Theatre in Dublin. But by the look of this backstage shot, taken as four of the performers get ready for their big night, the evening's success was not a foregone conclusion. There appears to be a serious discussion about - not surprising, really, in a dance show - something to do with feet. The joy of the picture is its sense of fleeting intimacy. The camera takes us right into the scene, closer even than the woman - a mother? a teacher? - who is hunkered down in front of her young charges. The dancers themselves are a set of variations on the theme of youthful intensity. On the left of the four, a fairy-like blonde figure gazes coolly at the kerfuffle in a "glad it's not me" sort of way. The girl on the right looks cross, or maybe baffled. But it's the two in the centre of the picture who grab our attention. One with foot up, one with foot down. One with hair up, one with hair down. One as serious as a George Orwell novel, the other transported by delighted laughter as she twists her foot into the most pliable of ballet poses. There's a lesson in that somewhere as we head, with trepidation, into 2013. But we'll settle for an "awwww".

Published -29/12/2012

Published: June 26th, 1984
Photograph by Peter Thursfield

Baby boomer

We've all heard of baby boomers - but this is ridiculous. Belfast, 1974. A British soldier runs a gigantic gizmo over a sleeping infant to check whether it has been up to no good with explosives. The baby, pudding-faced in innocent slumber, is blissfully unaware. A woman, holding the child's protective blanket in her hand, smiles at the photographer, every inch the proud mother - or proud grandmother. Behind the woman's left shoulder, on the other side of the street, two soldiers are questioning an individual who looks uncannily like Daniel Day-Lewis playing Gerry Conlon in the film *In the Name of the Father*. Without knowing to which side of the loyalist-nationalist divide the people in the photograph belong, there's really no way of knowing whether that smile is as relaxed as it appears. A scant two years after the Bloody Sunday confrontation in Derry, Belfast was a divided city. Alongside this four-column image, which appeared on March 20th, a report from the National Council for Civil Liberties expressed concerns about the erosion of civil liberties in the North following the Emergency Powers Act and the Special Powers Act.

Another story on the same page found the British army finally admitting the presence of SAS troops in the province after years of denials. A third recorded the protests of a 76-year-old Armagh farmer and his wife who had been pulled roughly out of bed in the early hours and made to lie on the ground outside in their nightclothes while their home was searched. All this against the background of an IRA bombing campaign that featured every kind of explosive apparatus, from a pipe bomb to what is euphemistically known as a "victim-triggered device". Under the circumstances, any smile at all seems like a small miracle. **Published -29/10/2011**

Published March 20th 1974
Photograph by Ciarán Donnelly

On the dotted line

If you reckon there's more than a touch of Antiques *Roadshow* about this shot, you're not far wrong - the woman on the right looks as if she has just been told her necklace is worth a fortune. We're certainly in high-and-mighty places. The occasion is the auction of the contents of Luttrellstown Castle, Co Dublin, on September 27th, 1983. The lady wielding the pen is Mrs Brinsley Sheridan Bushe Plunket, aka Aileen Guinness, daughter of Arthur Ernest Guinness; the castle was a wedding gift from dad in 1927. Here, she is simply autographing a catalogue for a punter. In fact, she had already signed the property over to a consortium, to be transformed into a luxury hotel - which is why we all associate it with the über-bling wedding of Posh and Becks in 1999. Aileen Sibell Mary Guinness was no stranger to bling. Born in 1904, she was the eldest of three glamorous Guinness sisters and a party animal extraordinaire. As chatelaine of Luttrellstown she set up a nightclub in a dungeon, and throughout the swinging 1960s was famous for "floor parties" at which everyone sat around and ate on the floor. Guests included Princess Grace of Monaco, David Niven and Ronald Reagan. Anyone who couldn't drive home was put up in one of the myriad bedrooms and woken at 11am by a liveried footman bearing a Pink Special - that's a Bloody Mary to you and me. They were, at least, a jollier bunch than the castle's original inhabitants. The land on which it sits, near Clonsilla, was "gifted" to sir Geoffrey de Luterel by king John of England around 1210. By the 17th century the family owned most of the immediate area - and made itself highly unpopular in the process, to the extent that at one point, the name of the building was changed to distance it from the Luttrell legacy. Luttrellstown has had a chequered time in recent years. It has been owned by millionaires JP McManus and John Magnier, has been refurbished, has opened and closed and is currently operating as a golf resort and country club. Liveried footmen are not, sadly, included as standard.

Published -12/11/2011

Published: September 27th, 1983
Photograph by Pat Langan

Geldof receives award from UN

When we think of Bob Geldof we tend to think famine, not food. But he did, as the song famously said, try to "feed the world" - and sure enough, here he is, getting an award from the UN's Food and Agricultural Organisation. A great honour - although not quite the Nobel Peace prize, for which the punk musician turned famine fund-raiser, instigator of Band Aid (1984), Live Aid (1985) and Sport Aid (1986) was nominated, unsuccessfully, twice. The UN award was presented by then taoiseach Dr Garret FitzGerald, and his inimitable wife Joan, who both appear to be enjoying themselves to the hilt. Geldof's expression is more ambiguous. He made no secret of his distrust of politicians and bureaucrats, although he was prepared to make an exception in the case of Dr FitzGerald - who had, in truth, gone all rock and roll the previous July when he made an appearance on RTÉ television to drum up dosh for Live Aid and announce a government contribution of £250,000. When a viewer phoned in to offer £5,000 for his tie, the taoiseach promptly undid his high-class knot and happily spent the rest of the show with his top button undone: a real sartorial no-no for politicians at the time. Perhaps, despite his protests to the contrary, Geldof would have liked to get the Nobel prize. Few in Ireland would say he didn't deserve it. Live Aid was an outstanding international gesture. But it also helped re-orient Ireland's position on the world stage. And it was a big hit at home, too; three million Irish viewers tuned in to the concert broadcast. By the end of the evening, RTÉ's £500,000 target had been doubled; by the end of the week, the figure had risen to £2.5 million, which tripled in the months that followed - a massive outpouring of generosity in a country crippled by high taxation, unemployment and emigration **Published -12/11/2011**

Published: October 17th, 1986
Photograph by Peter Thursfield

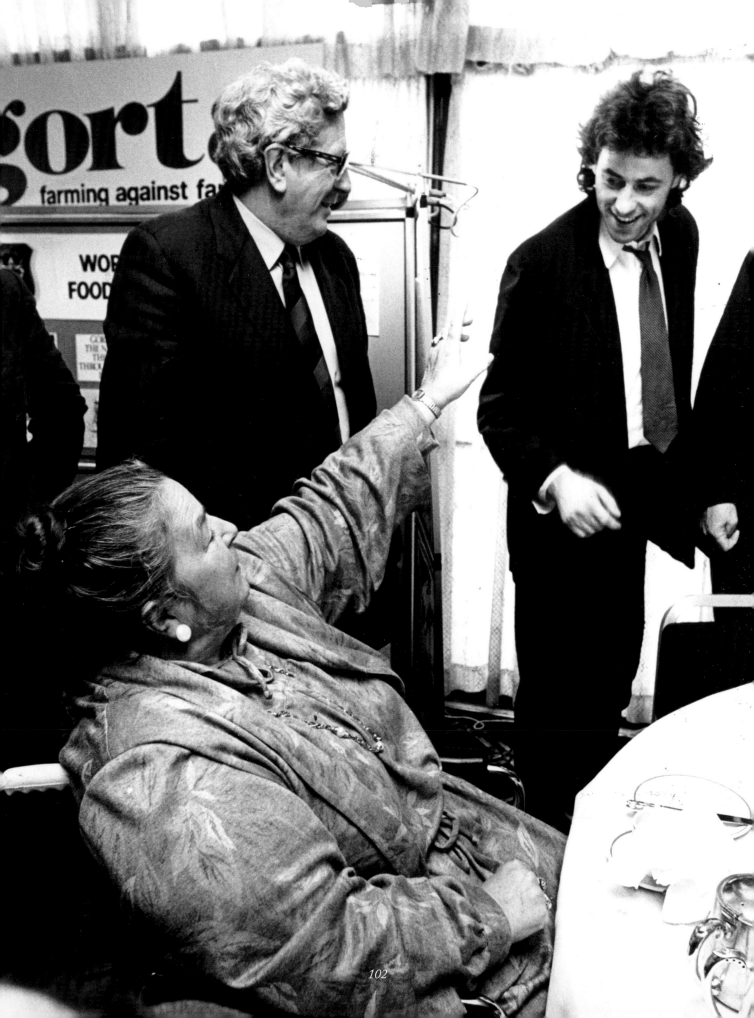

102

Tammy comes to town

There are many guilty pleasures to be had from the foot-stompin', finger-lickin' TV soap drama *Nashville*, currently showing on More 4 on Thursday nights. Not least of these is that the scriptwriters have clearly been told to mention "the great Tammy Wynette" in every episode – just in case viewers are too busy line-dancing around in their dressing gowns to notice any parallels between the fictional Rayna James and country music's real-world first lady. When she arrived into Dublin airport in March 1991 for a week of concerts, Wynette was certainly dressed for the role of upmarket diva. There's not a single chequered square in the singer's immaculate head-to-toe monochrome outfit, complete with race-day hat. As for that sassy expression, wouldn't you love to know what she was saying to the photographers? The year after this picture was taken, Wynette would get into a very public slanging match with Hillary Clinton, aka Mrs Bill, who told a television interviewer: "I'm not sitting here as some little woman standing by my man like Tammy Wynette." Wynette was incensed. She had never stood behind anybody, she pointed out, though she did notch up five husbands, 11 number one albums and *Stand By Your Man* is still one of the bestselling singles by a woman in the country music genre. But she never did get the fairytale happy ending beloved of TV soaps. Wynette suffered from serial health problems, including numerous surgical operations which left her addicted to painkillers by the 1970s. Look a little closer at the image – at the painfully thin arms and the loose skin under her right elbow, for instance – and the shadows of that darker drama can be clearly seen. It was quite a life. Even after her death in 1998 a the age of 55, Wynette was exhumed in order to ascertain the exact cause of her demise. Phew. I'm off to watch another episode of *Nashville*. It's all Zen-like serenity by comparison.

Published - 09/03/2013

Published: March 21st 1991
Photograph by Eric Luke

High fliers

Heading away for Paddy's weekend? Chances are, if you're flying off somewhere, you may be passing through Stansted airport. We used to speak about the airport as if it was on the outskirts of the equatorial rain forest. Nowadays, of course, we all know the layout and whereabouts of Stansted as intimately as the layout and whereabouts of our own living rooms. Thanks to Ryanair, right? Wrong. Aer Lingus got there first, as this photograph from the day of the airline's inaugural flight to Essex, EI444, proves. At that stage, Ryanair was still based in Luton and didn't shift its centre of operations to Stansted for another three years. The aim of the picture, presumably, is to encourage punters to sign up for this voyage into the unknown. But imagine arriving at check-in desk 20 to find the larger-than-life singer Colm Wilkinson towering over petite Aer Lingus hostess Elma Peters, looking as if he's about to grab that bunch of chrysanthemums and break into a song from *Les Miserables* at any minute. The original Jean Valjean, Wilkinson had been feted on both sides of the Atlantic for his role in the musical, which opened in the West End in 1985 and transferred to Broadway in 1987. He's giving his airline role plenty of welly, too. The hat, the mad eyes, the trenchcoat; it's all a bit Inspector Clouseau. Good fun so long as you're not the on-duty air hostess, worried that Wilkinson is going to scare away the paying passengers. And what were they paying? Thirty five punts each way, increasing to 45 a month later. A quarter of a century later, you can still fly to Stansted from Dublin, with Ryanair, for about €47. Meanwhile, the airport itself – the UK's fourth busiest, with 18 million passengers passing through in 2011 – is shortly to be sold to Manchester Airports Group for £1.5 billion. Not bad for the edge of the equatorial rain forest. **Published 16/03/2013**

Published March 2nd, 1988
Photograph by Jack McManus

A blooming great honour

Turning Japanese – was Garret turning Japanese? I really think so . . ." If you don't remember the dreadful 1980s pop song by The Vapours whose chorus ran something along those lines, lucky you. You will, however, remember the former taoiseach, leader of Fine Gael and long-time columnist with this newspaper, Garret FitzGerald. Just in case your memory needs a nudge, FitzGerald was a man of many talents. He spoke fluent French. He was vastly knowledgeable about some of the most desolate events in recent European history. He was also an economist, a barrister, liberal thinker and all-round Good Egg. In this image he is bending his head so that the then Japanese ambassador, Yoshifumi Ito, may confer upon him the poetically-named Order of the Rising Sun, Grand Cordon. You may smile. Actually you might as well, since everyone in the photograph is clearly enjoying themselves – with the possible exception of FitzGerald's wife Joan, seated on his right holding the scroll which presumably accompanied the honour, her expression betraying mild unease. Maybe she's wishing she had chosen a more sparkly cardigan for the occasion, given that the wife of the Japanese ambassador, Sumie Ito, has turned up in an asymmetrical stripey outfit which is of another sartorial order altogether. Mrs Ito, meanwhile, is applauding with great enthusiasm – but looking in the wrong direction. Maybe there's a piece of Noh theatre going on in another corner of the room or something. The Order of the Rising Sun is a serious honour conferred on relatively few people since it was established in 1875 by Emperor Meiji. Clint Eastwood has one. So had the late Kenyan environmental activist and Nobel Prize winner, Wangari Maathai. (Oddly, both Maathai and FitzGerald died in 2011). A decade ago the Order of the Rising Sun, Grand Cordon was renamed – even more poetically – Order of the Rising Sun with Paulownia Flowers. Will taoisigh present and future come into bloom one fine day? We'll have to wait and see.**Published 30/03/2013**

Published June 23rd, 1976
Photograph by Paddy Whelan

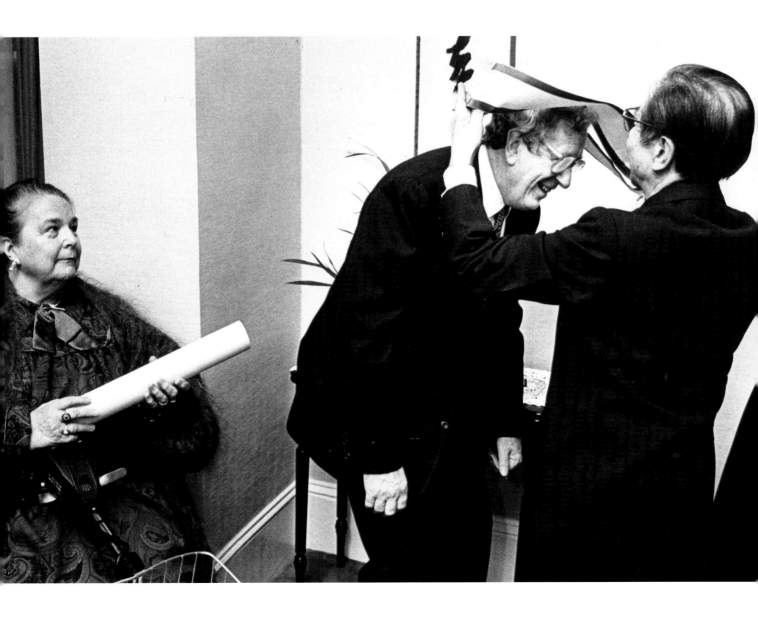

Three men and a lady

There was no expense spared the day the cast of Samuel Taylor's rom-com *The Pleasure of His Company* were taken across the road from Dublin's Gaiety Theatre to St Stephen's Green, to be photographed in the company of the local wildlife. It was a pretty upmarket cast, too. The lady attempting to make friends with the duck is Dinah Sheridan, more generally known as "the quintessential English rose" – and at the height of her fame, in 1976, for her role as Jenny Agutter's mammy in the 1970 movie *The Railway Children*. Watching her are a trio of debonair gents. On the left, we have Wilfrid Hyde-White, his lived-in face familiar from a million British comedy films. Stage centre, looking particularly spruce, is David Langton, who was best known at the time for his role as Lord Bellamy in the ancestor of *Downton Abbey*, *Upstairs Downstairs*. On the right is Douglas Fairbanks jnr - who, having been out-swashbuckled on the big screen by his dad, Douglas Fairbanks snr, took to the stage and made a decent fist of his theatrical career. To judge by their outfits the quartet hadn't set out to feed the ducks. They were doubtless strolling to lunch in some salubrious establishment on the periphery of the Green and had agreed to do some publicity shots while they were all dolled up. But nobody had quite bargained on the duck. It's not the prettiest duck in the world – in fact it's something of a shaggy duck story – but it waddles in and proceeds to steal the show. And all those celebrity actors? Well, for a change, they just have to take second billing. **Published - 30/03/2013**

Published: June 23rd 1976
Photograph by Paddy Whelan

Garden Variety

It's like an Irish Zen koan: water and land, sunlight and shadow. Or one of those tick-the-boxes magazine quizzes. Which personality type are you: lady in summer dress skipping gaily over rocks, or gentleman in suit proceeding cautiously across bridge? The lady in our picture is Madelaine Jay, owner of Mount Usher Gardens, in Ashford, Co Wicklow. Clearly at ease on her Japanese pond, she is leading the chairman of Bord Fáilte, Martin Duffy, in a merry dance to announce details of the first Wicklow Garden Festival. Duffy appears to be taking things rather more slowly, perhaps mindful of his high-gloss shoes, perhaps taking in the pond life. Despite their very different body language and their yin-and-yang outfit – she all brightness right down to her shoes, he in more funereal black – the photographer has caught the pair in almost identical pose, mid-step with right hand and right foot raised, marching as if in unison. Add in the clarity of the light and the reflections on the surface of the water, and you have a picture that sings: "It's summer! Get out into the garden!" You may have to wait for the last of the snow to clear first. But it's not too early to plan a visit to the Wicklow Garden Festival, still blooming every year from April through to September. Like any self-respecting perennial it has colonised the neighbouring counties as well, featuring some 33 gardens across counties Dublin, Kildare, Wexford and Carlow. Meanwhile, if it's still snowing as you read this, the cafe at Mount Usher – now run by Avoca – is a cosy spot for lunch, whatever the weather.
Published 06/04/2013

Published May 2nd, 1990
Photograph by Joe St Leger

Breaking news

In the spring of 1985, concern was growing at the crime rate in Dublin. There was controversy over the introduction of one-man buses, and the singles charts were prone to domination by such dismal ditties as Foreigner's *I Want To Know What Love Is*, or Elaine Paige and Barbara Dickson's *I Know Him So Well*. Crimes against music, some would say. However, change was in the air. New kids on the dance block were doing something called "breakdancing", ably demonstrated in our photograph by five members of the Dizzy Footwork breakdancing team – John Mansfield, Pat Daly, Brian Waters, Alan Dunnigan and Daniel Tracey – who were strutting their stuff on O'Connell Street in Dublin as part of International Youth Year. The photograph looks so much like a bunch of guys dressed up in 80s gear for a stag night, that it's quite hard to take it seriously. I mean, take a look at those buffed-up hairdos and snazzy sweatbands. And the general level of mugging from the lads – although to be fair to John Mansfield pictured on the far left, he's doing *Walk Like An Egyptian* a year before the song was even a twinkle in a record producer's eye. None of which is to deny the group's physical and/or musical prowess. Indeed, the Dizzy Footwork Dance Academy is still going strong, bringing a variety of new moves to dancers in south Dublin across an energetic range of genres. Breakdancing, however, is no more. If you Google it you will be redirected to an article about b-boying, where you will learn that the term breakdance – an invention of the ignorant mainstream media, apparently – has now been replaced by "breaking". Which is performed by b-boys, and even b-girls, collectively known as breakers. Now that's what I call breaking even.

Published 06/04/2013

Published May 2nd, 1990
Photograph by Joe St Leger

Into Africa

It may be a largely forgotten conflict nowadays, but in the early 1960s, many Irish families were all too aware of the ongoing hostilities in the newly independent Republic of Congo, to which some 6,000 Irish soldiers went as UN peacekeepers over four years. This image shows the advance party of the 33rd Infantry Battalion at Army Headquarters on the eve of their departure. In the front row, from left, are Sgt John Mullins, Moate, Co Westmeath; Comdt Patrick Keogh, Quarter Master, Adare, Co Limerick; Lt Col RW Bunworth, Cobh, Co Cork (commanding officer of the battalion, who did not travel with the party); Comdt Kevin O'Brien, Kildare, second command unit; Sgt John Bowe, Portarlington. In the back row, from left, are Sgt Michael Fenlon, Athlone; CQMS Patrick Dillon, Kilmacrennan, Co Donegal; Coy Sgt Michael Maher, Littleton Co Tipperary; CQMS Patrick Murphy, Middleton, Co Cork and CQMS Alfred Taylor, Dublin. The men gaze steadily at the camera, giving an impression of organised calm which belies the ferocity and chaos of the battles to come. Look more closely at the faces, though, and you can detect subtle variations on the official theme of unruffled stoicism. Actually, it would be no surprise if some of the soldiers in the picture are wondering whether their heavy woollen tunics and trousers might not be a tad OTT in a country where the average summer temperature – even in peacetime – reaches a whopping 30 degrees. No doubt their colleagues from the 32nd Battalion, who had already left for the Congo, had already reported back to this effect. Within 12 months of this photo being taken, Irish soldiers had served with distinction in such incidents as the Siege of Jadotville and the Niemba ambush. Nine Irishmen and 25 tribesmen were killed in the latter battle, which is commemorated every November at Cathal Brugha Barracks in Dublin. A total of 26 Irish soldiers died before the peacekeeping force was withdrawn in May 1964.
Published 20/04/2013

Published August 9th, 1960
Photograph by Eddie Kelly

Costume drama

Perched amid a plethora of pleats and stripes, her legs primly crossed in regulation ladylike 1950s fashion, this woman was one of the first Irish designers to make it on the international scene, making clothes for Jackie Onassis and the Rockefellers, designing crystal and pottery for Tiffany's and appearing on the cover of *Life* magazine. Sybil Connolly was born in Wales in 1921 to a Welsh mother and an Irish father. The family moved to Waterford, where young Sybil attended a convent school. At the age of 17 she went to London to study dressmaking, but returned to Ireland when the second World War began in 1939. By the time Ireland held its first international dress show in 1953, Connolly was a star. In our photograph she is dressed smartly but conservatively in pencil skirt and flowery blouse – the uniform of the independent working woman. She is looking somewhat critically at the dress to her right: perhaps it doesn't quite match up to the drawing she holds in her hands, though to the casual eye its tiny waist and immaculate bodice are almost uncannily perfect. But then, perfection is the name of the game here. The photo achieves an almost mathematical symmetry – in fact, the whole visual ensemble strikes the eye as a series of triangles. The jubilant spreading glory of the dress on the dummy echoed in the soft fall of the beribboned confection spread beneath Connolly's left hand - and again in the inky gleam of the dress on the far right of the picture, which appears black but might, of course, be any colour, even a strong red. The word "hourglass" springs to mind. No wonder Connolly disapproved of trousers which, she declared, were "only for riding". One can only imagine what she might say about tracksuits and trainers.

Published 27/04/2013

Published June 13th, 1953
Photograph by Jack McManus

Workers united

After his party's mournful showing at the Meath East by-election, we would love to be able to give the Tánaiste, Eamon Gilmore, something to cheer him up. Really we would. This picture, however, probably isn't it. Unless it makes him smile to see this younger self, all baby face, slim shoulders and earnest expression? Ah, well. We were all baby-faced once upon a time. This picture is really, however, a picture of another sort of face altogether – namely, a snapshot of the ever-changing face of the Irish political left. Taken at the Workers' Party conference in the winter of 1987, it features the party leader, Tomás Mac Giolla, flanked by Mr Gilmore (a mere county councillor who has yet to be elected to the Dáil) and – on the right – the TD Proinsias De Rossa. The document upon which they are all so intently focussed is a 44-page assessment of the shortcomings of the Irish taxation system. Determined to make tax reform a major issue in the forthcoming election campaign, the party aspired to reduce the tax bill of PAYE workers by 10 per cent (hooray) and transfer the burden to "farmers and the self-employed" (boo). In the photo, the body language of the three men sends a clear message. We stand (or, in this case, sit) shoulder to shoulder on this issue, it says. It was a rare moment of unity in the party's somewhat mercurial history. Once known as Sinn Féin the Workers' Party, it became the WP in 1982. Ten years later – five years after this picture was taken – Proinsias De Rossa left to form Democratic Left. Which, in turn, would merge with Labour in 1999. On this occasion, however, the trio are singing from the same hymn sheet as fervently as Pavarotti and Co ever did. And look at the headline on that document's front page. "Tax the Greedy, not the Needy", it declares. To which most of us taxpayers – not the greedy ones, obviously – would still utter a heartfelt Amen. **Published 04/05/2013**

Published January 24th, 1987
Photograph by Paddy Whelan

Kings of the Castle

Is it *Ripper Street*? Is it *Foyle's War*? No. It's the real thing. Once upon a time in Dublin city, we had real people doing real things rather than pretending to be all historical as a backdrop for the latest oldie-goldie television drama series. And here are three smiling Dubliners going about their real-life work – as messengers, aka orderlies, at Dublin Castle. Despite the smiles it seems that in 1953, nobody was living happily ever after at the Castle. "Take a look at the right-hand top corner of our picture," says the caption on this front-page 'Times Pictorial' story. "The crumbling stone, the crooked windows, the bulging walls . . ." Many of the Castle buildings had been condemned as unsafe and unhealthy, so a £4 million reconstruction was in the pipeline. "The picture is of buildings in the Upper Castle Yard," our story continues. "In the foreground are some of the messengers who will have to re-learn their way around the Castle when the reconstruction job is completed." Thanks to those gentle smiles, the light streaming across the courtyard and the photographer's meticulous attention to detail, the image is uncommonly vivid. Look at that beat-up box, and the string tied around the parcels carried by the man on the right. The casual way in which the man on the left has slung his messenger bag across his left shoulder. You can almost feel the warmth of the sun on the basket of the three-wheeler. Despite all the hoo-ha about reconstruction and re-learning, these men don't look bothered in the least. They look about as relaxed as it's possible to look when you're a civil servant involved in staging a photograph for a newspaper. Come to think of it, they're playing their parts as competently as any highly-paid extras from a telly drama. *Ripper Street*, eat your heart out

Published - 11/05/2013

Published: October 3rd 1953
Photograph by Dermot Barry

Sister act

There are acting families and there are acting dynasties – and then there are the Cusacks. They're more like a force of nature, especially in the annals of Irish theatre. Our photo shows Sorcha, Sinéad, and Niamh Cusack with Michael Colgan of Dublin's Gate Theatre, understandably jubilant at having secured the services of three first-rate female actors – and sisters into the bargain – to play the eponymous leads in Chekhov's turbulent play *Three Sisters*. The women seem delighted by the prospect. Flanking Colgan, Sorcha – on the left of the frame, clad in jumper and baggy corduroys – and Sinéad, slightly snazzier, mug happily at the photographer. Niamh, too, is in fine form for a woman who's wearing what looks suspiciously like a pair of outsized culottes. But what's happening on the right-hand side of the picture? Cyril, father of all the Cusacks and one of the most successful Irish actors of all time, looks as if he belongs to a different production altogether. Seated in a curlicue armchair, he might be posing for a formal portrait were it not for the cup of coffee in his hand and the ever-so-slightly raised eyebrow – which suggests that he is about to join in the general merriment. Given that the combined CVs of the Cusack sisters would run to a book the size of the Old Testament and that they have always done their own thing, artistically speaking, it's great to see them all together, and about to launch into the serious work of rehearsals for a play which finds three siblings marooned in a garrison town somewhere in the Urals. Sister act, and then some. **Published - 18/05/2013**

Published: March 5th 1990
Photograph by Tom Lawlor

Many young men of Mountjoy

What's this? A gathering? A music session at the Willie Week? A flat-cap reality- TV extravaganza? Actually it's the third annual drama presentation from Mountjoy Prison in Dublin, a production of John B Keane's *Many Young Men of Twenty*. The inimitable playwright himself is at the centre of the action, clutching a pint and surrounded by the cast, all of whom were members of Mountjoy Drama Project in 1988. Set in the back room of a pub this musical play, which deals with themes of unemployment and emigration, might appear to be tailor-made for a prison production. In particular, the irony of the chorus line from its title song, "many young men of twenty said goodbye", would not be lost on the prison population. Over the past 25 years Mountjoy prisoners have won high praise for their stagings of all sorts and conditions of theatrical pieces – including Shakespeare's *Othello* and *The Winter's Tale*. Here they are clearly getting on well with the Kerry playwright, who was throughout his life an outspoken advocate for the individual's right to freedom of expression, no matter what the social circumstances. And the range of expressions in the picture is, accordingly, rich and varied. Most of the actors are gazing at John B, presumably as directed by the photographer. Over his left shoulder, a pair of comedians are gurning at the camera. To their left again, in the background, is a man doing barman-type things and ignoring the whole shenanigans altogether. The guitarist, the ukelele player and the bodhran player appear to be holding, rather than playing, their instruments for the duration of the photo-shoot. Under the playwright's pint, however, the man with the tin whistle is lost in his music, his eyes closed in effort or ecstasy. It places him at the centre of the image, artistically as well as physically – the very incarnation of the transformative power of art. **Published 06/04/2013**

Published May 2nd, 1990
Photograph by Joe St Leger

Still waters run deep

All of the photographs chosen for publication in this column are, by definition, remarkable in some way. The captions are a different matter. Captions tend to be pretty deadpan. It's a caption's job to tell the reader who is doing what to whom, where and when. With these archive pictures – especially pictures which didn't make it into the paper at the time – captions often amount to a couple of names scratched down by a photographer in a hurry. We find them stuck to the back of the image with yellowing Sellotape; that's if the Sellotape hasn't dried out, in which case the caption may be missing altogether. But some, such as the paragraph which accompanied this photograph on page three of the *Times Pictorial* magazine in November 1955, are absolute gems. It is worth, therefore, quoting in full. It reads: "Some people think that one drink which goes well with a nice bit of goose, or with a nice bit of something else or, indeed, without a nice bit of anything else at all, is a drop of poteen. A Mayo farmer thought so and set up a still in his kitchen. He was well on the way to providing a nice long drink for himself, he had two buckets and a stone jar full when the guards arrived . . ." To which there is really nothing one can usefully add, except to give the names of the guards who are holding on to the still as if worried it might – goose-like – suddenly up and fly away. On the left, Garda John Morrissey looks as if he wishes he were somewhere else. On the right, Garda John Byrne also has a slightly uncomfortable air. But Sergeant Joe O'Brien, standing beaming in the middle with a proprietorial hand on each barrel, appears to be delighted with the outcome of the raid. As well he might be. The still is a miracle of DIY technology; a work of abstract art, almost. A nice bit of goose, indeed. **Published - 08/06/2013**

Published: November 5th 1955

127

Insuring against monotony

Tedium (n): the state or quality of being tedious; origin mid 17th century, from the Latin *taedium, taedaere*, 'to be weary of' ." The journalist and civil rights campaigner Nell McCafferty has always been one of our liveliest and most articulate commentators on matters cultural. But in this photo she outdoes even herself, providing an eloquent definition of ennui without raising so much as an eyebrow. The occasion is a meeting of the Insurance Institute of Dublin's Discussion Circle, which Ms McCafferty – along with the former minister of justice, Senator Patrick Cooney, also pictured – has come to address in the autumn of 1977. If anything, Senator Cooney looks even less rivetted than his co-panellist; he appears to be on the point of falling asleep. Far be it from this column to suggest that the discussion circle really was mind-bogglingly tedious. Maybe the pair are actually so fascinated by what is being said that they are, literally, petrified in the present moment. More likely this was one unrepresentative moment from a lively and varied evening. Still, the expressions on those two sleepy faces are hugely recognisable, are they not? We've all been there. Maybe not to that particular meeting, but to one very much like it. Oh, yes, indeed. According to some tantalising scraps from the online archives of the Insurance Institute of Ireland, the Dublin Discussion Circle was a wide-ranging, even provocative affair. It was founded by an Englishman, Percy Williams, who spent two decades in the world of Dublin insurance between 1910 and 1930. Mr Williams's insurance career then took him to Birmingham. But in a letter to the chairman of the Dublin Discussion Circle in 1943, he wrote; "I am still deeply interested in all that goes on in the Circle and it is a great pleasure to me to know that it remains so active and that it continues to prosper." Indeed. Although, looking at our photo, "active" is not the first word that springs to mind.
Published 22/06/2013

Published October 18th, 1977
Photograph by Tom Lawlor

A rural scene that's dead and gone

Once upon a time this would have been the archetypal romantic image of rural Ireland: the lone turfcutter, his barrow piled high, his craggy face creased in concentration. Not any more. Last year's bitter battle over the closure of 53 raised bogs in order to preserve peatland habitats for birds and plants turned Ireland's boglands into something much less like a John Hinde postcard and much more like a Magnum photograph from a war zone. News reports showed eco-activist groups such as Friends of the Irish Environment and the Roscommon TD Luke "Ming" Flanagan facing each other at dawn across serried ranks of agricultural machinery. Our photograph, it should be said, dates from three decades ago and is all legal and above board. It shows champion turfcutter Joe Daly from Tyrrellspass, Co Westmeath, in action during the second All-Ireland Turfcutting Championship at Meedin Bog near Tyrrellspass. As a photograph, it's fabulous. Look at the muscles on the man's arms, straining to keep his barrowful of bog from overturning. Look at his hat: he must be sweating, yet it's immaculate, straight, as pristine as if it had been carved out of marble. It's an almost balletic combination of balance and movement; yet that muddy front wheel is rolling right into the viewer's face in a slightly threatening way. Or is that threat an imagined one, driven by an instinctive woolly liberal conviction that it's wrong to cut bogs? Is it even okay to enjoy this picture – or is it akin to buying poached ivory or blood diamonds? The thing is, it's not wrong to cut all bogs: just protected bogs. It's also wrong to stop people from cutting bogs they've cut for generations, without appropriate consultation or compensation. It's a complex issue. But that's 21st-century life: complex. And once upon a time is gone for ever. **Published - 29/06/2013**

Published: June 27th 1983
Photograph by Jack McManus

A ruff ride

There would be a touch of "man bites dog" about this picture – if it wasn't for the fact that there's nothing amusing about those bandages. The photograph shows one of our most admired Olympians, Eamonn Coghlan, "resting in the Mater Hospital, Dublin" in December 1986 after being attacked by a marauding canine. If it was a cartoon, it would be hilarious. Dumb dog chases hapless human: the human in question being, as it happens, one of the fastest men on the planet. It would give the phrase Road Runner a whole new meaning. On the other hand, if you happen to be a world-class athlete, and both of your legs – plus one of your arms – are banjaxed in what was, presumably, a pretty scary incident; or if the person who has been attacked happens to be your husband or your daddy, well, that's a different story altogether. Check out the expressions on the children on the right of the picture. Suzanne Coghlan, aged eight at the time, and Eamonn junior, a baby-faced five, are definitely not amused by what has happened to their dad. Coghlan himself, however, is as relaxed as if he was lying on a sun-lounger by a pool somewhere. His wife Yvonne is also smiling. Which is probably why the picture, despite the potential seriousness of its subject, conveys a cheerful – even jaunty – mood. Kudos to the photographer: Coghlan's legs are the main focus of the image. But the strong diagonal line created by those sinewy shanks is softened by the way the three visitors are leaning, at an angle, towards the man on the bed. Thankfully, this story does have a happy ending. Coghlan went on to another Olympic appearance, making it to the semi-final of the 5,000 metres at the 1988 summer games. He is now a Fine Gael Senator and fundraiser for Our Lady's Children's Hospital. **Published 06/07/2013**

Published December 29th, 1986
Photograph by Jack McManus

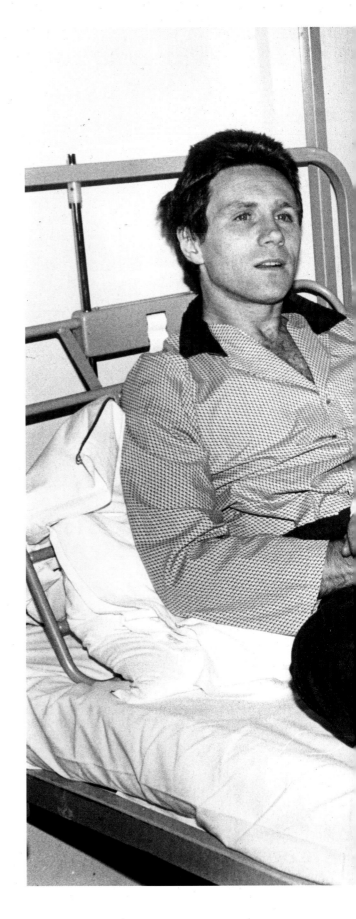

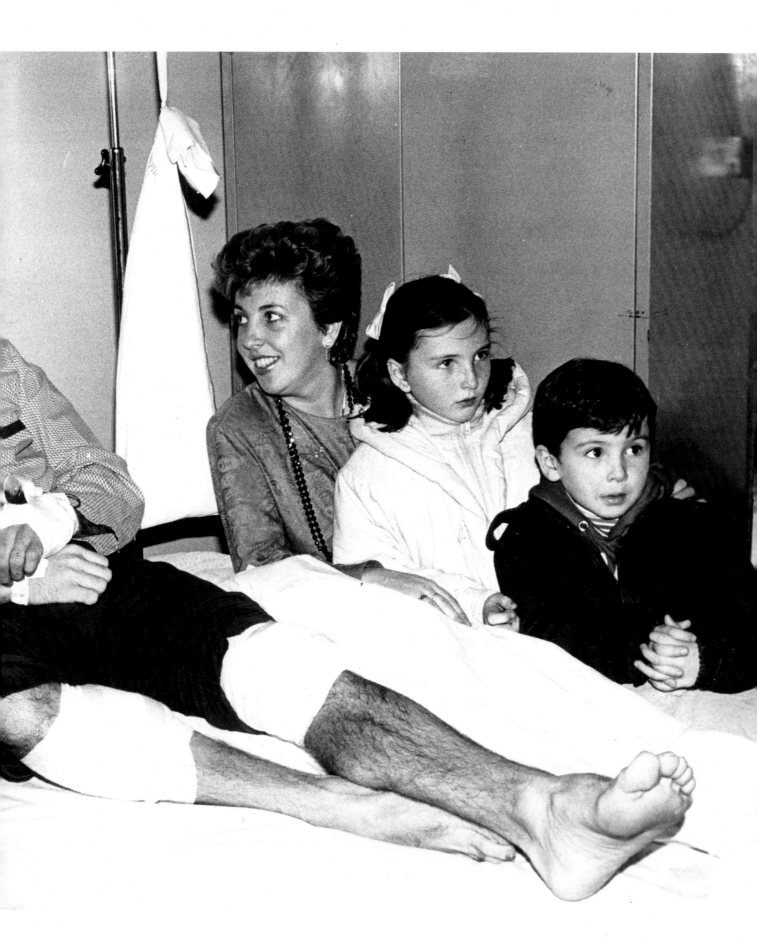

A real grande dame

She looks like she might have stepped out of the pages of a Beckett play. The gimlet eyes and haunted cheekbones. The severe, almost priestly garb. The androgynous figure. She also, somehow, looks older than her 57 years. When this photograph – accompanied by an admiring article, part of a series called, appropriately, "Portrait Gallery" – was published in the winter of 1955, Ninette de Valois would have been instantly recognisable to Irish Times readers. She was one of the most celebrated arts figures of the time; the founder of so many ballet schools that she is, even now, regarded as the godmother of British ballet. She was born near Blessington in Co Wicklow into an Anglo-Irish family, as the article has it, "Huguenot by descent and army and navy by tradition". Her birth name was Edris Stannus. More than 5,000 Huguenot families came to Ireland in the late 17th and early 18th centuries. Their descendants were to be influential in many areas of Irish culture: banking (the LaTouche family, who started Bank of Ireland); politics (Seán Lemass was of Huguenot descent); literature (Joseph Sheridan LeFanu, Dion Lardner Boucicault and Beckett himself). Among the many "de" names in the Huguenot cemetery in Dublin, however, you won't find "de Valois". That's because Edris Stannus's mother Lillith made it up. She took it from a novel by Alexandre Dumas senior about the French queen Margaret de Valois, then added "Ninette" because she felt it suited her diminutive daughter. Only her mother would have dared. As our photo shows all too clearly, you didn't mess with "Madame" Ninette de Valois. She has fixed upon the photographer the "dragon stare" for which she was famous. At the same time her pallor hints at a certain vulnerability, or fragility, behind the tough exterior. The position of her hands – the left relaxed but alert, the right like the claw of a roosting bird – suggests that she might fly away at any moment. She didn't, in real life. She lived to the ripe old age of 103. Diminutive or not, de Valois was the real grande dame deal. **Published - 13/07/2013**

Published: December 17th 1955
Photograph by Dermot Barry

The eyes have it

A child leans in to her grandmother, maybe to give her a kiss, maybe to share a joke. It's a universal and timeless gesture. It must have happened in neolithic cave gatherings. A 21st-century version happens in my house every time my four-year-old granddaughter lurches towards the computer screen in suburban Sydney, plaits flying, eyes glowing, to tell me about the dolphins she saw at Sea World, or the swimming pool her mum is going to put on the top of her birthday cake. It's rare for such an ordinary family moment to be recorded in a newspaper. But the granddaughter in our picture is Deirdre Sweetman, and her grandmother is Mrs Elgin O'Rahilly – sister of Kevin Barry. Not the Kevin Barry who has just won the IMPAC Prize with his wonderful novel City of Bohane, but the original Kevin Barry. The 18-year-old rebel who, as the well-known song has it – "gave his young life/ for the cause of liberty". The occasion was the launch of a biographical study, Kevin Barry and His Time, by the historian Donal O'Donovan, in the Kevin Barry Room. Which, in 1989, was still part of University College, Dublin but is now a recital space at the National Concert Hall. As noted above, the emotions recorded in the picture can never be dated. The affection in the grandmother's eyes, the excitement in the youngster's. The faces defy time, too. They might be reflected in some magical Harry Potter- style mirror; one old, one young, but still the image of each other. The two hands facing each other, one gnarled with age and experience, the other splayed out over the page of the book, bursting with childish energy. The light streaming in from the left, illuminating the older woman's immaculate bun and the girl's hair, which is also upstyled in a hairband. Do you know what, it's like an Irish, female, secular version of Michelangelo's God Creating Adam in the Sistine chapel. Or maybe, as a grandmother, I'm just biased. **Published 20/07/2013**

Published October 6th, 1989
Photograph by Peter Thursfield

137

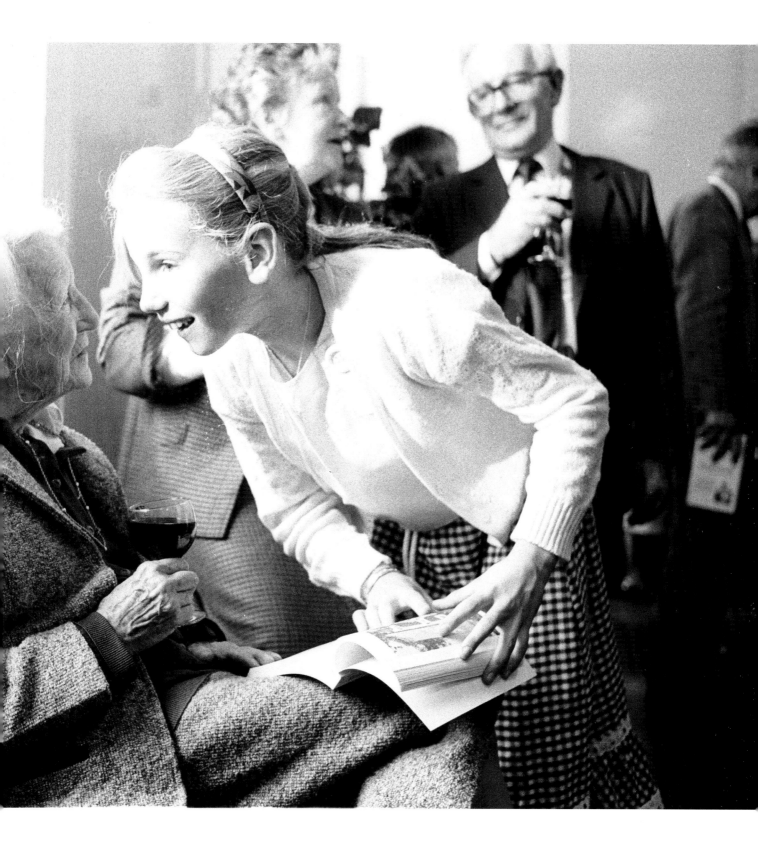

Cat with her skirt down

You've heard of somebody losing their shirt over a sporting event. Losing the head is also, alas, quite common. But losing your skirt, now – that's pretty unusual. Happily it doesn't seem to bother the Kilkenny camogie player Angela Downey, pictured in the autumn of 1989. And why would it? She has just scored a goal against Cork in the All-Ireland senior camogie final at Croke Park; and either she doesn't realise that she's skirtless or, more likely, she just doesn't care. Kilkenny won the match by 3-10 to Cork's 2-6. According to our reporter Pat Roche, this was Kilkenny's fifth successive all-Ireland victory, earning Downey her ninth all-Ireland medal. Her twin sister sister Ann, who scored a goal in the second half, also received her ninth all-Ireland medal on that day. The sisters are now legendary figures in Irish camogie and role models for young sportswomen and, indeed, sportsmen. In our photo Angela Downey's raised hands, clenched fists and grin of delight say, pretty much, all that needs to be said. It may not be a good look – though in fairness the pleated skirt, as worn by the player on the right of the shot with her back to the camera (twin sister Ann, perhaps? or not?) isn't exactly flattering anyhow – but Downey's lack of interest in how she looks is the mark of someone who is truly living in the moment. Skirts in sports are over-rated – but strangely tenacious. As another legendary sporting figure, Billie Jean King, once noted, "Ever since that day when I was 11 years old and wasn't allowed in the team photo because I wasn't wearing a tennis skirt, I knew I wanted to change the sport." Camogie players are still not allowed to wear shorts, but skorts – shorts with a discreet panel of fabric over the front, so they look like a skirt – are permitted. And they're a lot harder to lose. **Published - 27/07/2013**

Published: September 25th 1989
Photograph by Peter Thursfield

Flood brothers

First we baked, and then we sogged. This July was one of the most variable in Ireland in recent memory, with an unusually long spell of sunny weather (ie, longer than two days) followed by rainstorms which brought flash flooding in Dublin and Cork, the collapse of Clerys' roof, major disruption to Dart trains, 30mm falling on Glasnevin and lots more besides. Flooding in Ireland is not, of course, new. Did the lads in our photo wring their hands and check their apps and their Twitter feeds and their portable generic multimedia devices every five minutes and bemoan the state of the nation and the world? They did not. They just got on their bike, and got in their boat and generally got moving. As the caption on this image from the final day of 1959 puts it: "A touch of humour is lent to the seriousness of the Shannon flooding by this photograph: Joe Dunning cycles home on the Clonown road, near Athlone, as Edwin Hunter, Jimmy Reid, Harmon Murtagh and Michael Coen row alongside." The cyclist has a particularly angelic smile as he ploughs through what must – though it doesn't look like it in glimmering, artistic black and white – be pretty grotty water. His pals in the boat have more anxious expressions, perhaps concerned that they'll run aground, or tip over, on this river that-was-once-a-road. To the right and left of the picture, meanwhile, the flooded fields stretch away as far as the eye can see; the inundated hedgerows frame the action and draw the eye back to the horizon, where the distinctive towers of St Peter and Paul's church in Athlone are clearly visible. Maybe the smiles can be explained by the date. Maybe these five Athlone lads had a Christmas/New Year party to get to. These days, though, serious flooding episodes regularly recur in both winter and summer. Never mind the past: in this instance the future, in the shape of climate change, seems already to be upon us.
Published - 03/08/2013

Published: December 31st 1959
Photograph by KevinMcMahon

141

Cross–border craic

Handshakes across borders may seem like a recent phenomenon. But more than 40 years ago, on the steps of Iveagh House in Dublin, a Northern prime minister and a taoiseach were asked by photographers to "pose for just one more". And as the visiting prime minister, Captain Terence O'Neill, quipped to the taoiseach, Jack Lynch: "It's the old handshake act again." Tourism, tariffs, "the American curbs on investment in Europe", the metric system, foot-and-mouth precaution and cultural exchanges were among the matters discussed at a two-hour meeting between the two men and their delegations. It seems to have been generally good-humoured and positive, if not particularly revolutionary or insightful – except insofar as it happened at all. By the look of our photo, however, it was the women – Máirín Lynch, left, and Katharine O'Neill on the right – who showed the men a thing or two about how to have a good time. The smiles, the hand gestures, the apparently genuine outbreak of delight: they're all indicators that the two women were getting on like a house on fire. They had, in fact, more in common than their almost identical and resolutely non-stylish hats. Both had been married since the mid-1940s. Neither had been particularly keen to get involved in politics – born Katharine Jean Whitaker, Mrs O'Neill was a passionate plantswoman who, in later life, won the admiration of professional botanists – but once paired off with politicians, both were staunch in their support for their spouses and became almost as recognisable as their respective men in the public arena. And they both outlived their husbands; Máirín Lynch died in 2004 and Katharine O'Neill in 2008. Despite the laughter on this occasion, things would get serious in Northern Ireland before many months had passed. By the summer of 1968, Terence O'Neill was being pelted with eggs, flour and stones by members of the Woodvale Unionist Association, who disapproved of his "conciliatory" policies. He would resign the following spring and it would be a long, long time before the old North-South handshake act would come into play again. **Published - 10/08/2013**

Published: January 9th 1968
Photograph by Dermot Barry

Feeding time at the zoo

Ah, the delights of the endless, fun-filled summer holidays, boys and girls. Picnics in the park. Bathing at the beach. Nuts at the Zoo. Say again? Nuts? Zoo? It's hard to imagine in these days of political and zoological correctness; but once upon a time, Irish kids would prepare for a visit to Dublin's "Zoological Gardens" by putting on their best bib and tucker, turning down their ankle socks – and purchasing, from a licensed seller at the gate, a bag of what were known as "monkey nuts". In our photo this shy-looking young brother-and-sister pair, whose names are given as "Nancy and Nicholas Walsh of Kilkenny", are being handed a paper bag of nuts by the smiling stall-holder, James Russell. According to the caption, Mr Russell's family "has been selling nuts, fruit and sweets on this 'pitch' for the past 100 years". And yes, it is a plausible calculation, given that Dublin Zoo opened its doors in 1831. There's an innocence, even a sweetness about this shot which has to do with its total lack of pretension. The simplicity of the stall, with its stacks of paper bags, more than likely filled and rolled up by hand, and its covering of what looks like an ordinary domestic tablecloth. The hand-written sign. Then there's the immaculate turn-out of the children. They're dressed almost formally for their visit to the Zoo. No tracksuits or trainers for this family; the girl's beautifully cut coat and the boy's short trousers and jacket (a little too big for him, but there you go). There's not a brand-name or a designer anything in sight. These days, of course, if anyone handed a bag of nuts to a child they didn't know, they'd probably – given what we know about food allergies and anaphylactic shock – be arrested. And you're certainly not allowed to give monkey nuts to monkeys any more. Come to think of it, you're not even allowed to call them monkey nuts: though whether for fear of offending monkeys or nuts, nobody seems to be quite sure **Published - 17/08/2013**

Published: July 31st 1954

Michael D goes to work in Grand style

There's no denying our President, Michael D Higgins, has his own inimitable sense of style. But as this photograph shows, it's not something he has developed since his assention to the dizzy heights of Áras an Uachtaráin. Here he is, way back in the summer of 1994 – when he was merely a humble minister for arts, culture and the Gaeltacht – making what looks remarkably like a royal progress as he arrives, by barge no less, at his Mespil Road department in Dublin. He wasn't, however, just barging in by boat for the sake of looking good. The occasion was the setting-up of a task force to examine ways in which the Grand Canal from Ringsend to Lucan bridge might be developed and, in the parlance of these things, have its "resource potential maximised". The beneficiaries were to be tourists, community groups, commuters – almost in passing the article mentions the possibility of a Dart station being built on Barrow Street, as if such an outlandish eventuality could never happen – and even anglers. In those good old days of 20 years ago, there was money to be had for such projects; some £20 million in potential EU funding, according to the author of the piece, Lorna Siggins. Which doubtless explains the presence of two distinctly non-sailorly gentlemen to the left of the minister, dressed to the nines in the sort of attire not usually seen on canal barges. Higgins, by contrast, has at least had enough nautical nous to don a flotation vest. Still, his companions are commendably engrossed in whatever it is they're pointing out to the minister. And the folks who are actually driving the barge seem to be extremely relaxed. Nobody is tut-tutting or tsk-tsking or telling him to sit down, he's rocking the boat. For that, they would wait until he sailed into Áras an Uachtaráin. **Published - 24/08/2013**

Published: July 27th 1994
Photograph by Jack McManus

147

Man down but the game goes on

A prone body, an irate manager, a group of outraged GAA footballers: now where have we seen this before? Well, no offence to recent encounters, but this photo was taken during a Leinster senior football semi-final between Dublin and Meath in 1980. It shows the legendary Dublin player Ciaran Duff being treated for an injury. The equally legendary manager Kevin Heffernan has taken the opportunity to get on to the field and give his players a bit of encouragement. The Dubs among you may now be having a bit of an "aah" moment. The Dublin team of the late 1970s , aka "Heffo's army", were a force of nature. As Miriam Lord wrote in a tribute to Heffernan after his death in January this year, "We grew up in the shadow of Croke Park but never knew it until Heffo arrived. It was the place where country people went on a Sunday." Heffo's army changed everything. "They were exciting, they were sportsmen, they were winners and they were ours," Lord wrote. Not that Dublin's glory years were all sweetness and light. Look at the body language of the Meath player on the left of the photo, hand defensively on hip, and the grim expression of rangy Dubliner Alan Larkin, advancing towards the camera from the right. Duff himself, famous for crippling defences, not with rugby tackles but with sheer speed, was to have his own moment of madness in 1983, when he was sent off for stamping on a Galway player in a final summed up later as "a game full of thuggery and madness". As Dublin and Kerry prepare to step onto the field for the All-Ireland senior football semi-final tomorrow, the stakes for both counties are high. Fingers crossed for a high standard of football and a large dose of sweetness and light – even from the media punters – into the bargain
Published 31/08/2013

Published July 7th, 1980
Photograph by Pat Langan

Cruise goes native

Yankee dandy, reads the caption. It's the summer of 1991, and Temple Bar has been transformed into turn-of-the-century Boston. Striding through the streets of that make-believe city is the Hollywood megastar Tom Cruise, playing the part of an Irish immigrant in *Far and Away*. Fast-forward to the summer of 2013. The same Tom Cruise is presented with a certificate of Irishness – by our Tánaiste, no less. "We've checked you out and you're the real deal," Eamon Gilmore tells the actor. Life imitating art? Or just another bit of Hollywood-meets-The Gathering jiggery-pokery? Cruise, in fairness, has never hidden his Irish connections – his great-great-great-grandfather emigrated to the US in the 1820s. As the descendants of more recent Irish immigrants return from far and away for autumn gatherings around the country, however, this is a striking image to ponder. Cruise takes centre stage, of course, dressed as a 19th-century Boston gentleman, complete with bowler hat and three-piece suit. The tight framing of the photograph doesn't allow the viewer to see outside the film set. Such is the solidity of the (real) cobblestones and the (real) pair of horses in the foreground that the illusion is almost complete. Almost. Look at the expression on the face of the boy with the sweeping brush to the left of the image. What is he thinking, as he sweeps a heap of rubbish towards the feet of the great Tom Cruise? "Irish – yeah, right." Or: "He's not as small as he looks on the telly." Or: "What, this is the guy they've picked to play Jack Reacher?" There's nothing phoney about that sceptical look: it's Irish to the eyeballs. Some things – happily – never change. Cruise, meanwhile, appears to be delighted by the discovery that his Irish ancestry goes back to the Anglo-Norman ninth century. Or as he told an interviewer on US telly: "My ancestors owned a town called Hollywood." Ah, God love him. **Published 07/09/2013**

Published August 14th, 1991
Photograph by Joe St Leger

Where's a sleuth when you need one?

What's this – an Irish Miss Marple? The tweed coat; the string of pearls; the felt hat; the pensive, slightly mistrustful, expression. You could imagine this woman striding across a damp field in stout shoes, effortlessly solving the mystery of the missing paintings with one hand while knitting a tea cosy with the other. Art-loving readers may, by now, have recognised our subject. It's the painter and stained-glass artist Evie Hone, one of the most influential modernists of the early 20th century – one who, in fact, is credited with changing the face of Irish art. The picture was taken in the spring of 1947 when, as the story on page five of this newspaper explains, "Miss Evie Hone showed fourteen paintings in oil . . . at the Dawson Gallery, 4 Dawson Street. They are the Stations of the Cross." The writer adds that the painter's "combination of modernism and medievalism is strikingly original" and goes on to praise the policy of commissioning "native artists" to produce work to be used in churches around the country. "It would be a great pleasure to any traveller, to say nothing of the inhabitant, to enter one of our country churches to find it decorated by a native artist instead of the usual stereotyped substitute we see in most places." The article concludes: "It should be remembered that through Art we express the national conscience." Sadly, visitors to St Peter's and St Paul's Church at Kiltullagh, near Loughrea, Co Galway, will no longer find it decorated by Hone's superb set of Stations. Six of the paintings were stolen in June of this year, and may well have vanished into the eternal murk of the international illegal art market. The crime would have particularly grieved Hone, who was a devout woman, spending time in an Anglican convent before converting to Catholicism. A reward has been offered for the return of the "quite valuable" paintings. It may, however, take a Miss Marple to retrieve them. In the meantime, what price the national conscience? **Published - 14/09/2013**

Published: March 12th 1947

All human life is here

SOME photos are all-action affairs and can be read at a glance. Others exert a kind of slow-motion fascination; the onger you look, the more you ee. This is one of the latter. It was taken at the junction of O'Connell Street and Lower Abbey Street in Dublin, and shows a group of people waiting for the traffic to clear so they can cross the road. Behind them, a queue of buses is also waiting – and behind the buses, the hulk of Nelson's Pillar looms skywards. Why the picture was taken remains a mystery. None of the people are named; there was no news story associated with the image; yet it appeared on the front page of The Irish Times at a time when few photographs of any kind were published. Either somebody then liked it as much as I do now, or the annual summer news famine known as "the silly season" was already well under way. One way or another, the picture offers a compelling snapshot of an unremarkable Monday in Dublin in 1951. The random nature of the people makes it into a a kind of visual lucky dip. There's the stylish lady at the centre, wearing her gloves as ladies should, and a hat with a feather. To her right as we look at the photo, two girls in summer dresses stand arm-in-arm. One has a well-worn leather suitcase in her hand. To the left of the lady in the hat, a man walks into the crowd, his back to the camera. Over his left shoulder is the head of an elderly priest. On the far right, a little boy in short trousers is holding his mother's hand as they head on to Abbey Street just behind the –- well, what IS that thing on the stripy base? A Dalek? An alien listening device? Or just a bog-standard bollard? The longer you look, the more questions you have. Who are these people? Where are they going? We'll probably never know. Which only makes it all the more intriguing.

Published 21/09/2013

Published July 31st 1951

Past Victoria house to victory

The release of the feature film *Rush* is a throwback to the glamour days when the rivalry between James Hunt and Niki Lauda shot Formula One on to the front pages of glossy magazines. Well, anything those guys can do, we can do better. Have a look at the wacky racer pictured above. His name is CEC Martin and he's competing in a 1936 Cork road race over the Carrigrohane circuit. Our photo was taken at the first corner, named after the Victoria House pub. We don't know the photographer's name, but the words "Irish Times" are stamped in the bottom right-hand corner. To the right of the Alfa Romeo, a few hardy spectators can be seen on the footpath. The solidity of the pub, with its familiar "spirit store" signs inscribed on the windows, contrasts with the otherworldly sleekness of the car. The intensity of Mr Martin's focus also contrasts with the apparent stillness of his vehicle, which only adds to the weirdness of the vibe. Two years later a grand prix race on the same circuit was won by the French superstar Rene Dreyfus. Our motoring correspondent described the scene as Dreyfus roared to victory: "A low, powerful, light-blue car with the tints of the French tricolour slashed in a thin ribbon of paint from its nose to its tail, sped like a comet at over 140 miles per hour down the straight, flat concrete of the Carrigrohane road." Glamour, or what? This is one of the oldest photographs we've found in our archive. We are indebted to Colin James of Waldovision Films for drawing it to our attention, and to Alan Cavanagh of the Munster Vintage Motor Cycle and Car Club for identifying the driver. The club marked the 75th anniversary of the 1938 Grand Prix with a commemorative rally earlier this year, and a DVD featuring previously unseen film footage of the race, background information and fantastic photographs – some of which were rescued from a skip by an eagle-eyed club member – can be purchased from corkgrandprix.com

Published 05/10/2013

Published May 16th, 1936

Hair-raising weather

All the pictures in this slot are, frankly, worth a thousand words. But sometimes we come across an image that is so eloquent that there isn't a lot to say about it except: Wow! Look at this, guys! Such a photograph is today's bright and breezy study of a moment captured by Frank Miller on O'Connell Bridge in Dublin on the first day of February – technically the first day of spring, though it hardly ever feels like it – in 1990. We could offer a scientific analysis of the situation along the following lines. Wind: the movement of air caused by pressure differences at the Earth's surface. Ireland: a rock perched at the north-western corner of Europe, right in the path of Atlantic storms. Result: a more than average number of bad hair days for Irish heads. As the season of mists and mellow blusteriness blows in once again after one of the sunniest summers for many a year, we'll all become reacquainted with that storm-tossed feeling. Despite being wonky with wind, however, the heads in our photo manage to exude an air of youthful energy and enthusiasm. In fact they give a new meaning altogether to the phrase "a shock of hair" – not to mention the more technical hairdressing term "upstyle". There's an almost musical movement across and down the picture, from the semi-solid shape of the young man's mane, its asymmetric edges reflected in the angles of his shirt collar, to the wispy strands of the young woman's locks, mirrored by the misbehaviour of her scarf. And, incredibly, despite or maybe because of the buffeting, they're smiling. All together, now: "Always look on the bright side of life . . . dee dum, dee dum dee dum dee dum."

Published 12/10/2013

Published February 2nd 1990
Photograph by Frank Miller

159

Stick around and laugh a while

Ah, yes. The flowers that bloom in the spring, tra la. This picture shows The Hothouse Flowers performing in the first-floor window of the late, lamented, HMV shop on Grafton Street in the spring of 1988. The band had planned to busk outdoors, on the street, by way of a pre-publicity stunt before the release of its debut album, People. But word got out and some 3,000 fans turned up, prompting a hurried change of plan. There's a wonderful innocence about this celebrity frenzy from the days before Facebook and Twitter – before celebrities, almost. Look into the right-hand panel of the window (the one which reads Next cafe Espresso, with its elongated s's) and you'll see a group of those same fans, craning to get a look at their heroes. The window itself is a kind of modernist version of the sort of triptych you might find in a church. Something to do with those stern geometric shapes, perhaps; the triangles formed by the three panels and the phalanx of square tiles underneath. From the left-hand panel, Hothouse singer Liam Ó Maonlaí salutes the crowd while Leo Barnes looks, and presumably sounds, seriously cool on saxophone. In the central panel guitarist Fiachna Ó Braonáin, wearing one of his trademark funny hats, offers a cheery thumbs-up. What are they singing? Probably their greatest hit, Don't Go, with its quirky bittersweet lyrics and theme of living for the moment: "while the sun smiles, stick around and laugh a while". True to their name, The Hothouse Flowers blossomed, then faded; by 1994 it was all over for the band. The individual members are still going strong, though. As, indeed, is HMV, whose return to our streets represents a triumph for music fans of all ages and tastes. Maybe one day they'll even be back on Grafton Street. **Published 19/10/2013**

Published April 19th, 1988
Photograph by Matt Kavanagh

161

Behan there, sung that

There weren't many people who could drink Brendan Behan under the table: the author of Borstal Boy was an imbiber of legendary stamina. The ballad singer Margaret Barry could, however, give the playwright and novelist a good run for his money. She often sang at the Brazen Head pub, where she was said to be the stronger pint-sinker of the two. Our photo shows the pair about to tuck into the plain black stuff. Behan is hard at work lining the old stomach while Barry bears the glasses; they appear to be sharing a joke with each other, and with the photographer. At first glance, bizarrely, they might be brother and sister. The noses, the hands, even the hair carries a resemblance, as does the air of mischief which fairly dances and sizzles in both pairs of eyes. But while music certainly links both Barry, who was recorded by everyone from Alan Lomax to Ewan McColl, and Behan, who needed little prompting to get up and sing, and who came from a musical family – his brother wrote the song *The Auld Triangle* while his uncle penned the national anthem, *Amhran na bhFiann* – they were not related at all. Behan, who shot to fame in the mid-1950s with his play *The Quare Fellow*, became a casualty of his own success as alcoholism got the better of him. Nevertheless, we seem to find him endlessly fascinating. A new play, Brendan at the Chelsea, written by his niece Janet and starring Adrian Dunbar as the inimitable playwright, will play Belfast, Dublin and Derry this month after a successful spell in New York. Barry is more of a neglected figure. Born into a Traveller family in Cork in 1917, she overcame a difficult childhood – her mother died when she was just 12 – to create a long and well-regarded career as a travelling musician in Ireland and England. Her voice was, and still is, quite remarkable. You can replay it on YouTube. But when is Barry going to get her own play? Eh? **Published 26/10/2013**

Published August 11th, 1961
Photograph by Gordon Standing

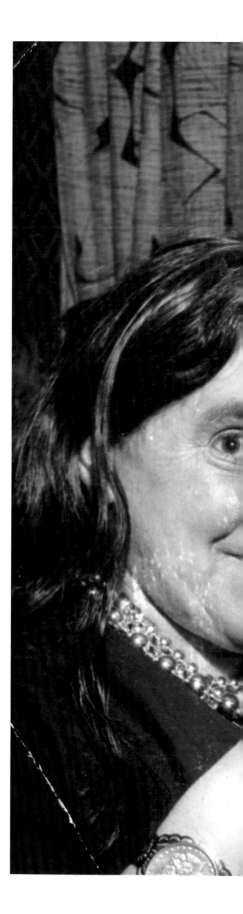

The borrowers

Been to a public library recently? Then you'll know all about the self-service machines where you can borrow and return books without the need to speak to a soul, let alone a living librarian. Plus the internet access, the online catalogue, the one-click digital app which allows you to download audiobooks to your devices and all the rest of it. Dalkey Public Library has its fair share of such mod cons these days and also, happily, an array of helpful staff. So familiar are its book-lined windows to anyone who walks regularly along Dalkey's Castle Street that it seems to have always been there; but as our photo shows, such is not the case. "The public library in Dalkey was re-opened yesterday after almost 20 years," reads the report in *The Irish Times* from November 1956. "The first public library was opened in Dalkey in 1901 and closed in 1937 because of proposals to extend the existing facilities by building new premises." Shot in black and white, the red bricks of the then "new" facade have an institutional air, reinforced by the cart in the foreground, complete with its Dickensian bucket and sacks. A shimmery reflection from the other side of the street adds a vaguely subaquatic seaside vibe. The ladies at the door of the library, however, are chatting away to their hearts' content. Are they on their way out, or their way in? Does that large shopping bag contain a week's supply of library books? Does the pram contain a baby? When the conversation ends, will one woman push the pram stage left and the other push the cart stage right? We'll never know. If you're thinking that public libraries are themselves a thing of the past, think again. Last year a survey declared that more than half of Irish people still use them regularly. Later, the library moved to new premises along the street. Now with a spanking new Central Library gradually taking shape in Dún Laoghaire on a prime perch above the harbour, it looks as if book-borrowing will be a feature of Dublin's cultural landscape for some time to come. **Published - 02/11/2013**

Published November 30th, 1956
Photograph by Jack McManus

Alternative energy

This picture of four young people standing by their tent, squinting into the sunshine, might be a simple holiday snapshot. What our photographer was recording on this occasion, however, was a camping trip with attitude. Our reporter, Dick Grogan, began his front-page story on Saturday, August 19th, as follows: "A fresh breeze blowing in from the Saltee Islands demonstrated an ample source of alternative energy as thousands of people arrived at Carnsore Point last night to begin a weekend of festivity and protest against nuclear power. The "festivities" on the southeastern tip of Ireland ranged from a gig by Christy Moore through an open-air debate about the rights and wrongs of the nuclear energy option to Mass celebrated by a local priest. The atmosphere, despite the seriousness of the topic, was akin to a music festival, with rows of tents, sausages being cooked over campfires – and plenty of rain. Our photo was clearly taken at a sunny moment. Most of the tents on display at the protest were of the standard, low-slung variety, but this young quartet cut quite a dash with their jaunty conical tepee, whose light walls fairly glow against the low Wexford horizon. The two young women on the right of the image are in tune with the iconic "look" of the protest movement, in maxis with scarves and beads. The woman on the left might have touched down from a different fashion planet altogether. Having somehow overcome the sartorial challenges of life under canvas, she smiles calmly at the photographer, her hair and vest top neat as a pin. The young man's gaze is elsewhere – perhaps on a nuclear-free future? The weekend was a huge success. Anti-nuclear sentiments became general all over Ireland – even at the ESB, whose plans for four nuclear plants at Carnsore vanished into the ether in 1981. Alternative energy began its move away from the counter-culture and into the mainstream. Debates about energy rights and wrongs are, of course, as heated as ever. **Published - 09/11/2013**

Published August 19th, 1978
Photograph by Eddie Kelly

Well, hello dolly

Movie merchandising – T-shirts, dolls, fridge magnets – that's a recent thing, right? Wrong. Here is Mr Walt Disney, way back in 1959, visiting Ireland for the premiere of his film *Darby O'Gill and the Little People* at the Theatre Royal in Dublin. And while he's at it, attempting to sell his King Brian of the leprechauns doll to the children of Ireland. The children in our photograph have clearly been dressed in their best clothes and told to make nice. They are, from left, Mary McNally, Anne Scott McLeod, Mark Upton, Dan Scott McLeod and Walter McNally. The US ambassador to Ireland at the time was RW Scott McLeod, presumably father to Anne and Dan. The girls appear to be chatting to the film magnate like seasoned diplomatic professionals. On the right, the boys look a little more sceptical. It's an interesting image because the kids look so – well, frankly, American. There's something about their grooming which makes this look less like an Irish newspaper picture and more like the sort of photograph a proud first-generation cousin might send home to the old country. A similar cultural disjoint applies to the movie itself – which is based on a series of books written by an English woman and popular in the US at the time. Disney, to his credit, did his bit for Irish kids with a special showing of the film for 1,000 underprivileged Irish children, who – according to our report – gave him "a great reception . . . when he went on the stage". Darby O'Gill and the Little People went on to become a classic slice of OTT Oirishery which is still a hoot to watch. It is memorable – among other things – for the moment when Sean Connery, playing a loves truck gardener, breaks into song. As for the King Brian doll, if anybody has one, wouldn't it be great to introduce him to Buzz Lightyear? To infinity and beyond, begorrah. **Published 16/11/2013**

Published June 25th, 1959
Photograph by Dermot Barry

Darkness at noon in Dublin's smog city

It was Dublin's scourge and Dublin's shame. An article in the *New York Times*, of all places, described the eerie substance which, by the late 1980s, was invading the Irish capital on a regular basis. It "creeps menacingly through doors and windows here", a columnist named Sheila Rule informed her readers. "It attacks throats and lungs …" She was talking about smog. This pernicious mixture of smoke and ash, caused by the burning of smoky coal, was at its most dangerous on still winter's nights. In 1982 a serious smog episode led to a spike in fatality rates across the city. December 1987 was a disaster. Measurements of more than three times the permitted EU limit were not uncommon. And so it was that at the end of November, 1988, the ladies in our photograph, from left to right: Mrs Pauline O'Hara, Mrs Bridget O'Hara and Mrs Mary Nolan, donned protective masks distributed by a local GP, Dr Conor O'Hanlon, to protest at government inactivity over smog levels. According to our reporter, Frank McDonald, on that weekend a blanket of smoke was hanging over Dublin for the third night in a row, "giving the streets an appearance of nightfall at noon". The invocation of high noon is striking because they have the look of superheroes in winter woollies, these fearless Dublin women. They may be sporting standard tweeds rather than capes and tights, but their eyes tell another story. They're spirited, and angry – and as they eyeball our photographer, also worldly-wise and more than slightly amused. In 1990 the sale of smoky coal was banned in Dublin, making smog an almost forgotten feature of city life. It wasn't all down to our terrific trio, of course. But kudos, ladies, all the same. If only James Joyce could see this image; he'd be sharpening his pencil for another chapter of *Dubliners*.
Published 23/11/2013

Published November 25th, 1988
Photograph by Peter Thursfield

Sister to sister

What next? First there's talk of Mary McAleese being made a cardinal at the Vatican. Now, Mary Robinson is hanging out with the saints already? Calm down. No need for panic. Reports of Mary McAleese's cardinalship appear to have been somewhat premature. And Mary Robinson is alive and well and beavering away at changing this world, never mind the next, with her tireless Foundation for Climate Justice. Mother Teresa of Calcutta has, it's true, passed on to the next world – but she's still only a Blessed, which is two steps away from actual sainthood. Our picture was taken in 1993, when the world's most famous nun dropped in at Áras an Uachtaráin. Having won the Nobel Peace Prize, Mother Teresa was a globally recognised figure. Robinson, by contrast, was just embarking on her international career, having been the first female President of Ireland for just three years. It is a smile-inducing study in female opposites. The lanky young head of state with her tousled curls and trendy two-piece, an immaculate row of buttons marching down its well-cut jacket, towering over the tiny, gnarled figure in her trademark blue and white robes, topped by a distinctly dodgy-looking cardigan. In retrospect – given the controversy which blew up around Mother Teresa towards the end of her life, the fortunes of the Catholic Church over a troubled decade and the Irish State's recent rebellions against Vatican hegemony – this rather sweet, amusing, even affectionate image could be read as prophetic of the triumph of the secular over the religious in Irish affairs. Far be it from us to do such a thing, but mischievous readers won't have missed the fact that the wall light over Mother Teresa's head acts as a kind of electric halo. If she gets bumped up to sainthood one of these days, remember: this is where you saw it first. **Published - 30/11/2013**

Published June 1st 1993
Photograph by Joe St Leger

The boy is back
in town

As Christmas shoppers in Dublin city centre may have noticed, Phil Lynott has been restored to his plinth on Harry Street. Paul Daly's statue of the legendary rocker stood proud for eight years before being knocked over and damaged last May. After a bit of a remix the statue is back in town, looking smarter than ever, its greatcoat hanging casually open, its hip cocked to strut its stuff, head crowned by a mop of eternally spectacular curls. No statue, needless to say, could come close to the charisma – or, indeed, the curls – of the man himself. Our photo was taken on the occasion of the first festival at Slane Castle in 1981 when, as the headline has it, "Music and sun leaves them slain in Slane". Thin Lizzy topped the bill at the festival, which also featured U2 and Hazel O'Connor. Some 25,000 fans danced, clapped and "sang along with the bands or sunbathed in front of the stage". Meanwhile, according to our coverage of the gig, "U2's publicity-conscious lead singer, Bono, delivered a warning from the stage to a lone bottle thrower. Reports might give the impression that everyone was smashing glass," he said. Gosh. Glass-smashing? What, no outrageous inappropriate behaviour later posted on social media and relayed all around the world? Happy days. The bould Phil – described by our reporter as "the eminence of Irish rock" – was in fine form. Our photo epitomises Lynott's style: the lazy smile, the hooded eyes, the confident gesture. The earring. The cool threads. The mop of curls. In fact, the picture is pretty much all about That Hair. At Slane, he dedicated a song to the people of Dublin. It was Trouble Boys. "I don't know anyone who'd stand face to face with the Trouble Boys," run the lyrics. We still don't know any musical celebrity who'd stand face to face with Phil Lynott. And the statue, with any luck, will outlive us all. **Published - 07/12/2013**

Published August 17th 1981

176

Times' eye on the radar in Howth

IS it a bird? Is it a plane? Is it a flat-pack dining-room table from Ikea? No. Our image shows, and I quote the original caption word for word, "part of the temporary radar station which has been built on Howth Head, Co Dublin, by the Army Air Corps. This photograph shows the huge aerial rotating on a lorry." If you ever find yourself doubting that we live in wildly sophisticated technological times, a single glance at the device will put you right. Because here's the thing. The installation of this delightfully ramshackle bit of kit was deemed exciting, not to say cutting-edge, enough to send an *Irish Times* photographer all the way to Howth to capture the moment for posterity. Little did they know how posterity – in other words, us – would giggle. So let's try and be respectful here. It may look like a Portaloo on the back of a Dinky toy, topped off by the skeleton of a flat-pack dining-room table. But the folks in our Defence Forces must, in the 1950s, have considered it a weapon to be reckoned with. Defensively speaking, things were very, very different in the Ireland of the 1950s. The shadows of second World War secret ops were still lying around, murky and ambiguous. We didn't even become members of the UN until 1955. And as the site of the scandalous 1914 gun-running affair – not to mention all those untamed cliffs and immigrant seabirds – Howth was one of the most potentially dodgy stretches of our coastline, and thus the perfect site for a bit of messing about with radar. Look at the rough ground beneath the truck and the low clouds in the background; the picture might as well have been taken in the high Arctic. To the right of the rear tyre as you look at the picture, meanwhile, there's a mysterious tall box with a slot – perhaps for putting coins into, to make the thing work? No doubt this 50-year-old contraption has vanished into the mists of military history. But thank goodness the photograph has survived. **Published - 14/12/2013**

Published: September 2nd, 1952
Photograph by Dermot Barry

Cuddle me up a happy Christmas

AWWWW. It's that time of year, isn't it? We're all in the mood for good news stories and small, fluffy animals. And these particular small, fluffy animals are so cute, they're off the end of the cuddle scale. They're also a good news story in their own right. In the summer of 1982 Niall, Aifric and Marie – yes, those are their names – were the first lion cubs to be born at Dublin Zoo after a catastrophic outbreak of TB had caused the zoo's entire population of lions and tigers to be put down five months earlier. The Causeway Safari Park at Benvarden, in Co Antrim, came to the rescue by donating a pair of lions, Natal and Natalie, who produced this terrific trio. In the years between then and now, scientific research has shown that when we human beings look at helpless little animals such as these spotty little kitties we experience a physiological response as our levels of the feelgood hormone oxytocin, *aka* the "hug hormone", go through the roof. Sadly, the years between then and now have also seen our species abuse and misuse the habitat of the world's cute, wild, and fluffy animals to the extent that both are disappearing at a rate of knots. (Check Dublin Zoo's excellent website if you don't believe me, dublinzoo. ie) As for large, ugly animals – well, nobody gets the hug hormone when they look at a shark, which is perhaps why we kill an estimated 100 million sharks, worldwide, every year. Sharks, meanwhile, kill about five of us. That's the way the eco-cookie is crumbling, just now. Don't let me ruin your awwww moment. But it might be worth finding out whether you can do something positive, however small, for some cute, fluffy animals – or some large, ugly ones – somewhere on the planet this Christmas. Before we run out of good news stories forever.**Published 21/12/2013**

Published June 4th, 1982
Photograph by Paddy Whelan

Reflections of a life on the stage

Oh, no it isn't! Oh yes, it is . . . the miraculous Maureen Potter, preparing to go onstage in the post-Christmas pantomime at Dublin's Gaiety Theatre in 1977. Maria Philomena Potter appeared in her first pantomime at the age of 10, in 1935. By 1977 she wasn't just synonymous with this festive art-form: as far as Irish theatre-goers were concerned, Maureen Potter *was* panto. This was long before the world of cross-dressing, big knickers and audience sing-songs was invaded by television celebrities and Jedward. But traditional pantomime has survived – even thrived – in the digital age. Astonishingly, it has changed very little. Sign up for one of the innumerable pantomimes on offer this festive season, and you'll find yourself shouting at a lumpy horse/cow/camel, singing daft songs and snorting at silly jokes – just as panto-goers did in the 1930s, never mind the 1970s. Our photograph has a narrative as full of twists as any self-respecting pantomime script. Beginning at stage left we see a small and apparently unremarkable woman in a dressing-gown. By the time we arrive at the reflection in the mirror on the right of the image, she is transformed: her eyes ringed with Cleopatra-esque kohl, her hair flattened, waiting to be topped with some outrageous wig. In between, the dressing table is crammed with the flotsam and jetsam of a long, long life in the theatre. Powder puffs, beads, photographs, figurines, letters, jewellery boxes, hairclips, spray cans, a miniature owl, a pair of glasses, a doll dressed in belly dancing gear and a card extolling the power of prayer. Not that Potter needed divine assistance on stage. She could sing; she could dance; and as she proved through her roles in Sean O'Casey's plays towards the end of her life, she was a fine tragic as well as comic actor. Maureen Potter died a decade ago, at the age of 79. But her legacy lives on. In fact, as this year's crop of dames and dolls shape up to step out, they may well hear a ghostly cry from somewhere in the wings. "She's behind you!" **Published 28/12/2013**

Published December 29th, 1977
Photograph by Dermot O'Shea

Dog day afternoon

Do your days lack direction? Are you stuck in the middle of the great river of life? Do you often wonder whether to turn right, veer left or just keep on keeping on? Are you even tempted (sometimes) to rush in and put the cart before the horse? This study of a group of five boys and their dog waiting for the traffic lights to change on Dublin's O'Connell Bridge serves as a wry comment on all the "New Year, New You" self-improvement stuff with which we're all bombarded at this time every year. From the body language of the boy seated just behind the horse, you'd swear those lights changed only once a fortnight. Hand clamped to cheek, head dramatically drooping, he has become The Thinker – and his friend beside him has caught the bug too. The lads in the seats behind are sharing a joke, perhaps at the expense of the youngsters who can be seen on the right of the photo, striding purposefully towards O'Connell Street – while at the back of the cart, a tousle-haired child wears a comically disgruntled expression as he dangles his legs into thin air. But the dog steals the show. Plonked in the middle of the road on his little sawn-off legs, he might have stopped for a bit of a chat with the horse, two old pals debating whether to go for a pint. Or maybe they're discussing new year's resolutions. Horse to dog: "Yeah. Lose weight, get fit and cut back on the fast food – especially those dodgy burgers – that's me. You?" Dog to horse: "Nothing much. Just drink less. Travel to new places. And keep off the auld Facebook, you know?" Because as even the dogs in Dublin town know all too well, that's pretty much what we all promise ourselves every year. And every year, we fall off the cart – sorry, wagon – and have to promise all over again the following year. And the great river of life rolls calmly on. **Published 28/12/2013**

Published January 18th, 1979
Photograph by Peter Thursfield

A perfect storm of a picture

We take newspaper photographs so much for granted that we often forget they don't just arrive, fully formed, on our pages and screens. Somebody has to frame the image, focus on the subject matter, get the light right. They have to be in exactly the right place at exactly the right time to capture an expression or an exchange or a gesture. And sometimes it all goes wrong. Usually when a photograph goes wrong it never sees the light of day. Pity the photographer in this shot, then, who had sallied forth bravely in the middle of a storm to bag some shots of spectacular waves crashing over the railings of the Victorian promenade at the seafront in Bray, Co Wicklow. She was well prepared, too. She had donned serious wellies and an even more serious waterproof coat. She strode fearlessly towards the raging sea, camera at the ready and suddenly – bang. A rogue wave exploded into the esplanade, catching her – like Doctor Foster in the nursery rhyme – in a puddle right up to her middle, if not much further north. Not only that, but the *Irish Times* photographer – positioned, cannily, slightly farther away – captured the action with a single smart click. Or maybe not. There could have been a dozen shots of breaking waves on this roll. Our photographer might have been drenched a minute earlier, and decided to retreat and wait for another victim. It might have been sheer luck. In any case, this is the image that made the front page, and rightly so. The foaming water. The despairing hunch of the drenched woman, hand raised in a vain attempt to protect her camera. The expression on the face of the bystander on the left, who – in his haste to get away – actually appears to be flying before the onrush of spray but who still turns back towards the sea, half concerned, half amused, to see what has happened. It all comes together to produce what is, in truth, a perfect storm of a picture..
Published 11/01/2014

Published October 18th, 1989
Photograph by Tom Lawlor

185

Silent upon a pique in Dublin

Sometimes newspapers can be endearingly strange. The photograph (right) appeared on page five of *The Irish Times* on February 10th, 1965, sandwiched between the news that Coleraine had been chosen as the site of the North's second university, and a report on the trial of a 36-year-old man accused of stabbing his 22-year-old wife to death. The subject of the portrait is the poet Ezra Pound, a friend of the Yeats's, who was later to be hugely supportive of James Joyce but who would also be remembered for his virulent anti-semitism. He was a controversial figure – and obviously, given this article, a 1960s celebrity. Our picture shows a man who is carrying the weight of the world on his shoulders. Gravity has certainly played havoc with that lined, angular, bearded face. On this occasion, however, the words definitively trump the image. Whoever wrote the following paragraph was a bit of a poet in his or her own right. "In the morning, before leaving Dublin, he sat silently and apparently lost in introspection while a photograph was taken. Ezra Pound, most eminent of poets, long has refused to talk to reporters and yesterday morning in his hotel he remained true to form. He sat, head hunched into his overcoated shoulders and walking stick in his hand, completely silent, completely unmoving. A woman came into the lounge to say that a car was waiting and said that it would be all right to take a picture. 'You can photograph him there if you like or outside, but he never speaks to reporters.' While the photograph was being taken . . . she explained that he had come to Dublin, to see Mrs WB Yeats. Now he was returning to Italy, where he continues to work on his Cantos. One was almost startled when suddenly Ezra Pound rose to his feet and soundlessly left the room." What more could we possibly say? **Published - 18/01/2014**

Published: February 10th, 1965
Photograph by Eddie Kelly

187

From one Kelly
to another

It is not such a big coincidence, given the prevalence of certain surnames in Ireland, but it makes for a nice story, not to mention a first-rate photograph. One of the most famous Kellys of them all, the fleet-footed film actor Gene – of *Singin' in the Rain* fame, among many other movies – comes to Dublin. The first person to greet him is a photographer from this newspaper – whose name, as it happens, is Eddie Kelly. "To record this meeting with another of the Kelly clan, Gene Kelly borrowed another photographer's camera and took his picture," reads the caption. A big theme in the paper for the first weeks of January 1959 had been the coming into force of what was called the Common Market. There were entire pages with no photographs at all, delving into the new customs regulations, internal tariffs and common pricing levels of agricultural products. Clearly, by Saturday 17th, it was felt that our readers needed a bit of light relief. It would be interesting to know whose idea it was, this bit of poacherturned- gamekeeper role-swapping. It's a fair bet it didn't come from Eddie Kelly – who was, in his later years at least, one of the quietest men on the planet – so the suggestion must have come from Gene. Which fits with his mischievous wink and sly smile. The picture is a black and white movie in itself. The texture is silky-smooth. Kelly's film-star looks – perfect teeth, check; perfect eyebrows, check – are, if anything, accentuated by the starry pattern on the background behind him and the dazzling check of his flat cap. The upturned collar of his overcoat, with its hint of detective fiction, adds a noirish touch. That camera is a bit of a star, too. The Graflex Speed Graphic large-format was the mark of a real "pressman" and about as high-spec as you could get. It would be interesting to know to whom it belonged – and whether our photographer was similarly equipped. Whatever kind of camera he was using, though, Eddie Kelly played a blinder.

Published - 01/02/2014

Published: January 17th 1959
Photograph by Eddie Kelly

Stars of the show

We're totally spoiled on the musicals front nowadays. We've just had *Wicked*, with its green witch and winged dragon. We're about to have a new *Fiddler on the Roof,* with Starsky himself, Paul-Michael Glaser, starring as Tevye. Come the end of March it will be the turn of *War Horse*, complete with those astonishing giant horse puppets. Two decades ago, expensive special effects certainly weren't the strong point of this production of *Barnum*. A few stars stuck on to the floor, a couple of dodgy-looking circus props, a forest of jazz hands. And that, pretty much, was it. There are those who would quibble with the description of *Barnum*, which tells the story of the American showman and humbug merchant PT Barnum, as a musical. A circus with a few songs thrown in, they'll say. The original Broadway production, however, starred Jim Dale and Glenn Close, while a later incarnation won an Olivier award for Michael Crawford. The production which came to Dublin in the spring of 1992 featured the bubbly blond actor and pop star Paul Nicholas. By comparison with his 1976 hit single *Dancing with the Captain (Doo Doo Doo Doo Doo)*, Barnum was a musical masterpiece. Not that our theatre critic, David Nowlan, was impressed. "Bah, humbug" was his considered verdict on the opening night. There need be no such critical reservations about Pat Langan's photograph. The clever angle of the shot conveys the upward sweep of those triumphant arms as smartly as any video clip. The picture is all movement, from the hoops in the hands of the performers through the series of circular lights across the top of the frame to the shiny round buttons on the costume of the young man in the foreground. Who, thanks to that same shooting angle, appears to be very tall indeed, cutting Nicholas – star of the show or not – down to size. It's a fair bet it won't happen to Paul-Michael Glaser. Unless of course he disappears behind his outsized Tevye beard .. . **Published - 08/02/2014**

Published: March 25th, 1992
Photograph by Pat Langan

Down safely from the misty mountain

It's always bad when people go missing in the mountains. But when a group of 18 children and five adults is awol in Co Wicklow for more than 16 hours at the end of February, well, that's a big news story. This particular story had a happy ending. All 23 walkers – members of Palmerstown Youth Club and their leaders – got home safe and sound on the morning of February 28th, 1994. Even so, from the number of worried faces in the crowd, the scale of the previous night's search operation is clear. Civil Defence workers joined the mountain rescue teams who were combing the hills. So did mountain rescue dogs from places as far away as Cork and Co Down. Even the ESB weighed in, supplying four-wheel drives to add to those of the Garda anti-terrorist unit. It turned out that, having taken a wrong turn in the mist, the group leaders had wisely decided to take shelter until first light. "I'd describe it like sleeping in a fridge without a cover," one of them told *The Irish Times*. "We piled the children on top of each other to keep warm and the adults created a barrier to protect them from the wind." It probably wouldn't happen now, in these days of mobile phones and GPS trail apps. But as any hill-walker will tell you, strange things can happen to phone signals in the hills. Hence the simultaneously warm and shivery feelings induced by the image. The contrast is also evident in the manly stance of the rescuer, who is effortlessly carrying a child in his arms and allowing himself a half-smile of relief. Yet his body language is irresistibly reminiscent of all those heartbreaking Pietà sculptures in which Mary cradles the dead Jesus. The rescued boy, for his part, is wrapped snugly in his blanket. But his eyes, looking directly at the camera, tell the story of a long and chilly night. And behind all those busy, efficient human beings and their equipment and gadgetry – right at the centre of the picture, and leading away to infinity – the misty, silent mountains have the last word. . **Published 15/02/2014**

Published March 1st, 1994
Photograph by Alan Betson

Strictly Old Time in Beaumont

Strictly Come Dancing, eat your heart out: anything you can do, we can do better. Flashing feet? Check. Straight backs? Check. Poised, elegant young dancers? For sure. The picture was taken at the Flora Millar Dublin Dance Championships – at the Amateur Old Time competition, to be precise – which was held at the Artane Beaumont Family Recreation Centre in the spring of 1988. We got in touch with Flora Millar, who was able to name three of the four dancers. On the left of the photo, Olive Cummins and her partner Terence Leonard; next to them are Sarah Power and her partner, whose first name is Derek but whose surname, alas, has vanished into the mists of memory. For those who are used to watching ballroom dancing in the lavish setting of a television studio, the functional concrete backdrop of the sports centre, with a basketball hoop just visible on the extreme left of the shot, might come as something of a shock. The members of the audience, meanwhile, are not all paying attention to the action on the dance floor. Some onlookers are clearly studying the moves with care. Some are directing their gaze elsewhere – possibly to other couples who have yet to dance into the photographer's line of vision. Still others appear to be ignoring the whole business. The circular movement in those skirts, however, is so graceful you can almost hear it as a waltz tune. "And, you know," says the irrepressible Ms Millar, who has now retired as a dance teacher but is still in great demand as a competition judge, "the fashion hasn't changed very much at all. I've just come back from the UK Championships in Bournemouth, where the dresses were very similar. Perhaps a little shorter – Audrey Hepburn length – and with a little less heavy decoration." At another competition, in Blackpool, she happened to meet none other than our pictured dancer Sarah Power, whose 10-year-old son was taking part in a competition called Champions of Tomorrow. Which just goes to show that someone is listening to that *Strictly* injunction to "Keeeeeep dancing . . ." **Published 22/02/2014**

Published March 14th, 1988
Photograph by Eddie Kelly

Nabbed in the nip

It was with great sadness that we learned of the death, a month or so ago, of Paddy Whelan. An *Irish Times* staff photographer for almost 30 years, Paddy was a gentle and reassuring presence. There were many occasions when, as a nervous young reporter, I turned up to a tricky assignment, only to be reassured when the cavalry turned up as well – in the shape of Paddy, armed with his camera, his big glasses and his even bigger smile. But as this picture from the summer of 1990 illustrates, he had a mischievous side too. It's the perfect publicity stunt. Bring a troupe of long-legged female dancers to the Forty Foot bathing place in Sandycove, wait for a short, wrinkly legged nudie man to show up, click, whirr, and – job done. The Gaiety Theatre must have known they were on to a good thing with this clever photoshoot for their show *Can't Stop The Music*. But they got an extra ooh, la la factor when Paddy was the man doing the clicking. The picture calls to mind the traditional "naughty" seaside postcards of Donald McGill, which were designed to provoke mild doses of shock and horror – as well as a smile – in the viewer. Here the naughtiness is located inside the image itself, with several of the women raising hands to their faces in exaggerated fashion, prompting readers to respond in kind. Given the controversy over the customs and practices traditional to the Forty Foot – long-running, and still ongoing even to this day – you could read the shot as a socio-political comment on the place's longtime banishment of women bathers. You could see it as irrefutable proof of the proposition that men should wear togs in the sea at all times – for the sake of the good name of our species. You could see it as an exercise in barefaced cheek. Or you could just think to yourself, guess what? From photographic heaven, Paddy Whelan is beaming benevolently on us still. **Published 01/03/2014**

Published June 14th, 1990
Photograph by Paddy Whelan

High fashion
in Arnott's

It may have been the "Swinging Sixties", but scary supermodels – they of the skeletal body and razor-sharp cheekbones – had yet to be invented. So Arnott's department store was way ahead of the posse when it hired this young woman to take part in its 1966 autumn fashion show. The caption reads simply: " 'Twiggy', a London model, wearing a blue boucle coat trimmed with Mongolian lamb . . ." It's a classic slice of *Irish Times* understatement. Twiggy was, in fact, *the* London model – and 1966 was the year she hit the big-time. Twiggy was born Lesley Hornby, but nobody remembers that. Along with the big eyes, long eyelashes and cheeky Cockney demeanour her nickname quickly became part of her legend. Her trademark, however, was that boyish haircut, which our photo shows off to perfection. In fact, swathed in the enormous fur collar – what size *are* Mongolian lambs, anyway? – the sleek blonde head, smooth and shiny as a seal, looks far too small for her body. And the angle of her neck is downright weird, giving Twiggy the appearance of one of those dolls which used to come on the back pages of girls' comics, with paper clothes which you could cut out and attach to the body with folding tabs. If you attached an outfit to a doll but failed to line it up properly, you ended up with something which looked not unlike this photograph. As for the dinky little shoes and pale ribbed tights – can you imagine any of today's supermodels setting out on the catwalk in anything so wholesome? Not that she's on a catwalk. She appears, rather, to be dancing on a table in the Arnott's cafe. In the years that followed Twiggy went on to make an even bigger name for herself with her own TV chat show, reality-telly judging spots and all the rest of it. For the past decade she has been doing television ads for Marks & Spencer, looking as sprightly as ever. The cropped hair, though, is no more. Wisely, she has accepted her growth from twig to mature tree. Published - 06/03/2014

Published: October 14th 1966
Photograph by GordonStanding

Bridge of beauty and a Liffey landmark

When she finally sets sail – she seems to have been in dry dock and covered with scaffolding for ever – Dublin's newest Liffey crossing, the Rosie Hackett Bridge from Hawkins Street to Marlborough Street, will be the city's 18th bridge across the river. What about the other 17? Few of us could even name them. (See how many you can nail down; there's a list at the bottom of this article). We can all spot the Calatrava Two – harp-shaped Sam Beckett and snazzy James Joyce – but as for the rest, it's one of those situations where, though we see them all the time, we rarely really look. If you walk along the river from the O2 to Heuston Station, zig-zagging across the river as you go, and take the time to study these extraordinarily diverse structures, you'll find a wealth of architectural detail to amuse the eye. And if you check out Dublin City Council's tribute website, bridgesofdublin.ie, you'll find stories about the building of the bridges to add to your enjoyment. The reconstruction of O'Connell Bridge in the early 1880s, for example, created disruption on a scale which puts the Rosie Hackett saga into perspective. The structure began life as Carlisle Bridge, designed by the Calatrava of his day, James Gandon, in 1791. By 1882 it had been remodelled and dedicated to Daniel O'Connell, whose statue can be seen soaring into the sky towards the right of our photograph. At the other end of the street, looming almost to the clouds, is Nelson's Pillar. In fact the most striking thing about the picture is the scene's profusion of vertical lines. The lamp posts; the pillars on the bridge itself; and the facade of Clery's, with the cupola on the roofline of the building opposite. Dublin, it seems, was a city of dreaming spires before An Túr Solais was more than a gleam in anybody's architectural eye. The bridges (east to west): Eastlink; Beckett; O'Casey; Talbot; Loopline; Butt; O'Connell; Ha'penny; Millennium; Grattan; O'Donovan Rossa; Father Mathew; Mellows; Joyce; O'More; Sherwin; Heuston.

Published - 15/03/2014

Published: January 20th, 1952

Outside her comfort zone at new Busáras

Whatever you might say about Busáras, you'd never accuse it of being a cosy sort of place. Its high modernist stone-and-concrete vibe doesn't encourage curling up comfortably in corners. Even before it was unveiled to the paying public at the end of October 1953, Dublin's spanking new bus station was the cause of much discussion around the city. Architects adored its glass facades and pavilionised top storey – designer Michael Scott was eventually to win the RIAI Triennial Gold Medal for his hard-edged, Le Corbusier-influenced confection – but local wags preferred to focus on the building's soaring costs: a million in old money, by the time it finally opened for business. Punters arriving in search of buses on that first day, however, found themselves puzzling over one design feature in particular. The building didn't contain any seats. Was it some kind of international (aka communist) design conspiracy? Or just a way of drawing attention to one of the world's most expensive terrazzo tiled floors? Were the seats in some way imaginary, or invisible, in some arty architectural comment on the meaning, or lack of it, of modern life? Actually no. The builders just hadn't got around to delivering them yet. And so it was that our photographer discovered Mrs J Smith of London perched on a distinctly unsalubrious-looking parcel trolley, belongings stacked neatly beside her, reading material in her immaculately-gloved hands, an expression of quizzical forbearing on her aristocratic face. According to the caption she is "waiting for her bus to Wicklow". She has, if the Aer Lingus bag is anything to go by, just come from the airport. And, by the cut of her tidy spectacles and neat hat, this was a woman who, having organised herself to the nines, didn't approve of builders not delivering seats at the required time. On the wall behind her the gaudy, faux-Celtic map of Ireland looks especially ironic, offering a wealth of destinations to a traveller who is, for the moment, going nowhere. Happily for generations of travellers ever since, the seats arrived two days later. Let's hope the bus had arrived long, long before that. **Published - 22/03/2014**

Published: October 21st, 1953
Photograph by Dermot Barry

A brush with spring

It was wishful thinking then, and it's wishful thinking now. March, we tell ourselves wistfully every year, comes in like a lion and goes out like a lamb – only for the lion to eat the lamb and leave us all in a miserable stew of wind and rain. But maybe – just maybe – spring is out there somewhere, waiting to give us a taste of balmy days and bright evenings. Meanwhile we can feast our eyes on this gentle, light-dappled study which, as published in March 1972, carried the caption "an artist at work in the spring sunshine in St Stephen's Green, Dublin, yesterday". She was determined, and probably experienced, this woman. She had prepared thoroughly for her day of painting outdoors, arming herself not only with easel and canvas but with a sturdy wooden box of paints and brushes. Whatever shade of green turned up in front of her, she was going to be able to cope. Meanwhile, she's taking no chances on the weather front. It may be a day of glorious spring sunshine, but she's remarkably well wrapped up. Her outfit is an entire paintbox in itself; spotted skirt, checked coat, paisley-patterned headscarf. This is a woman who does her own thing, on canvas and off. And her concentration is absolute; if she has spotted the photographer lurking behind her, she gives absolutely no sign. With any luck, that concentration held until she finished her task, and produced a successful painting in the end. The unfinished canvas in the photo holds a kind of promise which accords perfectly with the tranquillity of the spreading tree overhead, the curve of the brick surround, and the peaceful scene just visible on the other side of the hedge as people relax on benches in the sunshine. It's on the way. It is. Honestly. Even though, as another artist once put it, it seems like years since it's been here . . . **Published - 29/03/2014**

Published: March 22nd, 1972
Photograph by Dermot O'Shea

Compose an ode to old Parnell Square

The area around Parnell Street has become emblematic of the changes wrought by time on our capital city. It was the sight of its thriving ethnic hairdressers and restaurants which led many of us to realise the world had come to Dublin and was living here, happily getting on with its daily life, whether we knew it or not. It does us good to take a fresh look at our urban surroundings every so often. It's easier said than done, though. Happily help is at hand from the One City One Book selection for 2014, *If Ever You Go*. Edited by Gerard Smyth and Pat Boran and published by Dedalus Press, this generous fistful of poems about the city wanders the streets, peering through windows, visiting galleries and monuments and shops and – every so often, when it just can't help itself – breaking into song. It was a particularly evocative poem by Mark Granier which reminded me of the archive cityscapes we sometimes feature in this column. Entitled *A Photograph of Fade Street, Dublin, 1878*, it begins "The exposure, half a minute? Enough for light's breath/to cloud the glass . . . ." and goes on to talk about "the pair of women who stand talking with a third" and "children who whirr, sparrow across the street". Readers are invited to compose their own poem on the subject of this lively 1955 study of Parnell Square East. The street signs are a poem in themselves – a kind of litany of Dublin life at the time: Forte's Snacks and Ices, Hawkins' Tailors, The Anchor Hotel and, just visible to the right of the bus, the iconic Ierne Ballroom. And then there are the people. The man wheeling his bike, looking very serious; the woman freewheeling down the hill to his left. On the pavement, another woman raises her hand to her head, perhaps smoothing her hair after a gust of wind. And look at that group of men with the dogs at the bottom right of the scene. Dwarfed by an enormous lamppost, two of them are squaring up to each other in what must, surely, be an explosive moment. Poem? Sure it's an entire song cycle.

Published 05/04/2014

Published November 25th, 1955
Photograph by Jimmy McCormack

Portrait of a gentleman

Who said Ireland in the 1950s was a place of unremitting dullness? It may appear so, from this stiff-and-starchy photo of the 1954 Arts Council presenting to the millionaire Sir Alfred Chester Beatty, by way of thanks for his donation to the Irish people of his priceless collection of Oriental and Islamic art, a stonking great portrait of himself. It must be pretty awkward to pose in front of such a thing – remember Brian O'Driscoll's embarrassment under that mammoth "Thank you, Brian" banner at the Ireland-Italy game? But Sir Alfred smiles gamely at the camera, reflecting the hint of a smile in the portrait. If he has noticed that the man on the canvas is considerably slimmer, he gives no sign. The rest of the people in the photograph look unaccountably glum. They are named as follows: standing, left to right, Dr RJ Hayes, Professor Séamus Delaney, Mr Thomas McGreevy, the artist Mr Seán O'Sullivan, Dr N Nolan and Dr Liam O'Sullivan. Seated in the front row, left to right, John Maher, Mr Eamonn de Valera, TD , the taoiseach Mr JA Costello, Sir Chester Beatty, Miss M Gahan and Senator EA McGuire. On the face of it, it's a depressingly masculine gathering. But the anonymous- looking "Miss M Gahan" is in fact Muriel Gahan, feminist heroine, founder of the Country Shop and a tireless campaigner for Irish craftspeople, who now has a museum named after her at the Irish Countrywoman's Association premises in Termonfeckin, Co Louth. Meanwhile, back at *The Irish Times* of October 1st 1954, the picture is on a page which also features a story expressing Dublin Gramophone Society's delight with the latest Pye "Hi-Fi" record-player, *aka* the "Black Box" – a quarter-page ad for which instrument runs shamelessly alongside – a report on the (voluntary) limiting of dance hall licenses to 1 am in summer and midnight in winter, and a graphic account of the rampancy of myxomatosis in the Irish countryside. "Anyone who motored from Wexford to Dublin, through Carlow, saw motor-cars driving over dying rabbits . . ." Ireland in the 1950s: a place of unremittingly dullness? Not when you look closely.

Published 12/04/2014

Published October 1st 1954
Photograph by Dermot Barry

On holidays from The Troubles

As Easter approaches and thoughts turn to short breaks, beaches and holiday plans, it's hard to believe that once upon a time, children from Belfast were brought to Cork to give them a break from the stressful situation back home. The caption on our photo doesn't explain who organised the trip, and whether it was semi-official or a private event. It simply reads: "Children from Belfast who have been on holiday in Cork, enjoying a meal in the CIE Hall, Dublin, yesterday, before returning home." The young family in the picture has just gotten as far as the soup course. But to judge by the fact that one of the two pretty pigtailed sisters has already finished hers and the other is all smiles as she raises the spoon to her lips, it seems to be going down well. The sweetness of the shot – with the mother, on the left, feeding something to an appreciative baby – becomes positively poignant in the context of what was going on in the North. Four months after this picture was taken, 26 bombs went off in 80 minutes on what became known as "Bloody Friday", leaving 11 people dead and 130 injured. A 2004 film called *Mickybo and Me*, clips from which can be seen on YouTube, really captures the atmosphere of the time. Based on a stage play by Owen McCafferty, it's the story of two boys, one Catholic, one Protestant, who – inspired by a screening of *Butch Cassidy and the Sundance Kid* – flee Belfast for adventures in the countryside. It was made by the director Terry Loane, who, in an interview, told Donald Clarke that the story of the film partly reflected his own childhood. "I grew up in north Belfast during the worst of The Troubles and we used to go for holidays in Cork," he said. "Then we'd come back and, like in the film, I would lie in bed hearing guns and bombs go off. My brother and I used to just think: 'Why can't we live in Cork forever?' It seemed like an idyll." Maybe that's why the youngster in the middle of the shot has such a rapt expression on her face. Dreaming of Cork. Or just hoping for a second bowl of soup? **Published 19/04/2014**

Published March 22nd, 1972
Photograph by Dermot O'Shea

211

The calm before the gathering storm

AH, the razzmatazz of politics. The coloured balloons, the speeches, the flag-waving. The heady triumph of winning a general election. Or then again you could have politics, Irish-style. A man with a pipe looking at an ancient television screen upon which the image of another man is smeared in blurry black-and-white. Not for nothing, it seems, did they call Jack Lynch "The Reluctant Taoiseach". Hand in pocket, leaning on a chair, he hardly seems thrilled by the prospect of a second term as leader of the Dáil; indeed, he regards the face of his defeated rival, Liam Cosgrave, with the mildly disinterested air of a vegetarian watching a telly chef run up a spot of Beef Wellington. In reality, the election result had confounded pundits and politicians alike. The outgoing Fine Gael-Labour coalition had been widely predicted to bag itself a second term in office, thanks not least to the controversial rejigging of constituency boundaries known to history as "Tullymandering" after the then minister for local government, James Tully, who oversaw it. Fianna Fáil, for its part, drew up a manifesto which promised the electorate a string of financial "sweeteners" including the abolition of car tax and domestic rates. If only politics could take a leaf out of technology's book, and actually change for the better with the passage of time. If the Taoiseach's path to power strikes us as all too familiar, his telly has a fabulously retro look – as does the turntable which can be seen to the left of the screen. Shame we can't see what he had in his record collection. Abba? The Bee Gees? Rod Stewart? Or perhaps, to celebrate his election victory, The Eagles' song *Life in the Fast Lane*? It's far from the fast lane he is here. "The picture," recalls our photographer Peter Thursfield, "was taken at Jack Lynch's home on Garville Avenue, Rathgar on a beautiful June evening in 1977. There were only a few people in the house at the time and the atmosphere was calm." It didn't last. Lynch's second term in office was to prove stormy in the extreme, not least inside his own party. He resigned in 1979, paving the way for Charles J Haughey to become Taoiseach. Politics, Irish-style, would never be the same again.

Published 26/04/2014

Published June 18th, 1977
Photograph by Peter Thursfield